PRISM

LISTENING AND SPEAKING Intro

N.M. White
Susan Peterson

with
Angela Blackwell
Christina Cavage

CAMBRIDGE
UNIVERSITY PRESS

CAMBRIDGE
UNIVERSITY PRESS

University Printing House, Cambridge CB2 8BS, United Kingdom

One Liberty Plaza, 20th Floor, New York, NY 10006, USA

477 Williamstown Road, Port Melbourne, VIC 3207, Australia

4843/24, 2nd Floor, Ansari Road, Daryaganj, Delhi – 110002, India

79 Anson Road, #06–04/06, Singapore 079906

Cambridge University Press is part of the University of Cambridge.

It furthers the University's mission by disseminating knowledge in the pursuit of education, learning and research at the highest international levels of excellence.

www.cambridge.org
Information on this title: www.cambridge.org/9781316620885

© Cambridge University Press 2017

First published 2017
20 19 18 17 16 15 14 13 12 11 10 9 8 7 6 5 4 3 2 1

Printed in Dubai by Oriental Press

A catalogue record for this publication is available from the British Library

ISBN 978-1-316-62088-5 Student's Book with Online Workbook Intro Listening and Speaking
ISBN 978-1-316-62505-7 Teacher's Manual Intro Listening and Speaking

CONTENTS

SCOPE AND SEQUENCE

UNIT	WATCH AND LISTEN	LISTENINGS	LISTENING SKILL	PRONUNCIATION FOR LISTENING	
1 PEOPLE _Academic Disciplines_ Anthropology	The Life of a Businesswoman	1: Students introducing themselves 2: Two student presentations on famous people	_Key Skills_ Understanding key vocabulary Taking notes _Additional Skills_ Using your knowledge Listening for main ideas Listening for details Synthesizing	Syllable stress	
2 CLIMATE _Academic Disciplines_ Geography / Meteorology	How Deserts are Formed	1: A lecture about seasons 2: Student presentations about places	_Key Skill_ Using visuals to predict content _Additional Skills_ Understanding key vocabulary Using your knowledge Listening for main ideas Listening for details Synthesizing	Sentence stress	
3 LIFESTYLE _Academic Disciplines_ Anthropology / Sociology	The Age Wave	1: A classroom discussion about leisure time 2: Answering survey questions	_Key Skill_ Listening for main ideas _Additional Skills_ Understanding key vocabulary Using your knowledge Listening for details Synthesizing	Intonation in questions	
4 PLACES _Academic Disciplines_ Geography	Urbanization in China	1: A radio program about an app 2: Following directions in a shopping center	_Key Skill_ Listening for details _Additional Skills_ Understanding key vocabulary Using your knowledge Listening for main ideas Synthesizing	Stress in directions	

LANGUAGE DEVELOPMENT	CRITICAL THINKING	SPEAKING	ON CAMPUS
Subject pronouns and possessive adjectives The verb *be*	Using idea maps	**Speaking Skills** Countries and nationalities Vocabulary for jobs Introducing and starting a talk **Pronunciation** Word stress in sentences **Speaking Task** Tell your group about a famous person from your country.	**Communication Skill** Formal and informal language
Seasons Weather Colors *There is / There are*	Choosing visuals for a talk	**Speaking Skills** Describing photos Giving a talk Adjectives **Pronunciation** Sentence stress **Speaking Task** Describe photos of a place you want to visit.	**Communication Skill** Asking for clarification
The simple present • Statements • Questions Verb collocations	Using surveys	**Speaking Skill** Prepositions of time **Pronunciation** Simple present -*s* and -*es* endings **Speaking Task** Interview students for a survey.	**Study Skill** Time management
Vocabulary for places Prepositions of place The imperative	Interpreting maps and directions	**Speaking Skills** Giving directions Asking for directions **Pronunciation** Phrases **Speaking Task** Ask for and give directions in a college town.	**Study Skill** Recording and organizing information

UNIT	WATCH AND LISTEN	LISTENINGS	LISTENING SKILL	PRONUNCIATION FOR LISTENING	
5 JOBS *Academic Disciplines* Business & Management	Burj Khalifa	1: A formal conversation asking for advice 2: A discussion about job applicants	*Key Skill* Using your knowledge to predict content *Additional Skills* Understanding key vocabulary Listening for main ideas Listening for details Predicting content using visuals Synthesizing	Weak form *have to / should*	
6 HOMES AND BUILDINGS *Academic Disciplines* Architecture	Monticello and Jefferson	1: A radio interview about restaurants 2: A discussion about buildings	*Key Skill* Listening for reasons *Additional Skills* Understanding key vocabulary Using your knowledge Listening for main ideas Listening for details Synthesizing	Linking words	
7 FOOD AND CULTURE *Academic Disciplines* Sociology	Eating Insects	1: A classroom discussion about food culture 2: A student presentation on food culture and changing habits	*Key Skill* Listening for numbers *Additional Skills* Understanding key vocabulary Using your knowledge Predicting content using visuals Listening for main ideas Listening for details Synthesizing	Numbers with *-teen* and *-ty*	
8 TRANSPORTATION *Academic Disciplines* Engineering / Urban Planning	China's Modern Roadways	1: A talk about the London Underground 2: Two student presentations about traffic problems	*Key Skill* Synthesizing information *Additional Skills* Understanding key vocabulary Using your knowledge Predicting content using visuals Listening for main ideas Listening for details Taking notes	Years	

LANGUAGE DEVELOPMENT	CRITICAL THINKING	SPEAKING	ON CAMPUS
Have to / has to *Should* Comparative adjectives	Understanding criteria	**_Speaking Skills_** Asking for and giving opinions and reasons **_Pronunciation_** Weak sounds in comparatives **_Speaking Task_** Choose a person for a job.	**_Communication Skill_** Asking politely
Vocabulary for furniture Adjectives for furniture	Finding reasons for and against	**_Speaking Skills_** Reasons, opinions, and agreement • Giving reasons • Giving an opinion • Asking for an opinion • Agreeing and disagreeing **_Speaking Task_** Discuss ideas for a new café.	**_Study Skill_** Participation and classroom behavior
The simple past 1 • statements • *Yes/No* questions and short answers • Irregular verbs Vocabulary for food	Using pie charts	**_Speaking Skills_** Introducing a report Talking about surveys **_Pronunciation_** The letter *u* **_Speaking Task_** Report the results of a survey.	**_Life Skill_** Keeping healthy
Verbs for transportation The simple past 2 • More irregular verbs *Because / So*	Synthesizing and organizing information for a talk	**_Speaking Skills_** Describing a topic Describing a problem Describing a solution Describing results **_Pronunciation_** *-d / -ed* in regular simple past verbs **_Speaking Task_** Describe a transportation problem, solutions, and a problem	**_Life Skill_** Finding help

HOW *PRISM* WORKS

1 Video

Setting the context

Every unit begins with a video clip. Each video serves as a springboard for the unit and introduces the topic in an engaging way. The clips were carefully selected to pique students' interest and prepare them to explore the unit's topic in greater depth. As they work, students develop key skills in prediction, comprehension, and discussion.

WATCH AND LISTEN

ACTIVATING YOUR KNOWLEDGE

PREPARING TO WATCH

1 Work with a partner and answer the questions.
  1 Do most men and women work in your country?
  2 Do men and women have the same or different jobs?
  3 What do women in your country do in their free time? Do men have the same or different hobbies?
  4 What jobs and hobbies do the women and men in your home have?

PREDICTING CONTENT USING VISUALS

2 Look at the photos from the video. Circle the correct answer.
  1 The woman is working *in an office / at home.*
  2 The family is *happy / sad.*
  3 The view of the *city / country* is beautiful.
  4 The man likes to *ride his bike / run.*

GLOSSARY

busy (adj) when you are busy, you have a lot of things to do
exercise (v) to do an activity, like running or swimming, to make your body strong
relax (v) to be calm and comfortable
schedule (n) a list of dates and times that shows when things happen

10   UNIT 1

---

2 Listening

Receptive, language, and analytical skills

Students improve their listening abilities through a sequence of proven activities. They study key vocabulary to prepare them for each listening and to develop academic listening skills. Pronunciation for Listening exercises help students learn how to decode spoken English. Language Development sections teach grammar and vocabulary. A second listening leads into synthesis exercises that prepare students for college classrooms.

LISTENING

LISTENING 1

USING YOUR KNOWLEDGE

PREPARING TO LISTEN

1 Talk with a partner. When you meet people for the first time, what do you tell them about yourself?
  • your name?   • your last name?   • your family?   • your job?

Understanding key vocabulary
Before you listen, try to understand the key vocabulary in the Preparing to Listen exercises. These words will help you understand the main ideas of the listening.

UNDERSTANDING KEY VOCABULARY

PRISM Online

2 You are going to listen to four students talk about someone they know. Before you listen, read about two other students. Then write the words in bold from the texts in the chart below.

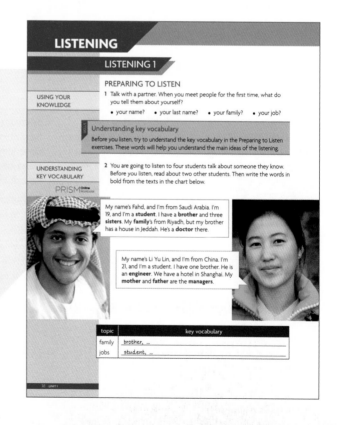

My name's Fahd, and I'm from Saudi Arabia. I'm 19, and I'm a **student**. I have a **brother** and three **sisters**. My **family**'s from Riyadh, but my brother has a house in Jeddah. He's a **doctor** there.

My name's Li Yu Lin, and I'm from China. I'm 21, and I'm a student. I have one brother. He is an **engineer**. We have a hotel in Shanghai. My **mother** and **father** are the **managers**.

topic	key vocabulary
family	brother, ...
jobs	student, ...

10   UNIT 1

PREPARATION FOR SPEAKING

REASONS, OPINIONS, AND AGREEMENT

1 ▶ 6.6 Listen to and read three parts of Listening 2. Notice the underlined phrases. Why do the people use them?

1

Dale:	OK, so we need a place for our new office. <u>What about here?</u>
Hakan:	Where?
Dale:	Downtown. <u>What do you think?</u>
Hakan:	Well, <u>it's a good place</u>. <u>It's near some good roads</u>. But ... <u>I don't think we should go there.</u>
Dale:	Oh? <u>Why not?</u>
Hakan:	<u>Because the buildings downtown are very old</u>. <u>They are cold in winter and hot in summer. They're uncomfortable places.</u>

2

Dale:	<u>What about here?</u>
Hakan:	The park?
Dale:	Yes. <u>It's quiet, and it's not far from a big road</u>. <u>What do you think?</u>
Hakan:	Hmm, <u>I'm not sure</u>. <u>It's pretty far from the town</u>. <u>What about here?</u> Near the train station?
Dale:	<u>The train station is good</u>. <u>It's good for travel</u> ... but <u>I think we should go to the park</u>. <u>The buildings near the train station aren't cheap.</u>

3

Hakan:	Now <u>what about the design?</u> <u>I think we should have a modern design with big windows</u>. <u>What about you?</u>
Dale:	Yes, <u>I agree</u>. <u>Big windows are good.</u>

2 Write the underlined phrases in the correct column of the table.

give a reason	give an opinion	ask for an opinion	agree or disagree

PRISM Online

PREPARATION FOR SPEAKING 141

---

3 Speaking

Critical thinking and production

Multiple critical thinking activities begin this section, setting students up for exercises that focus on speaking skills, functional language, and pronunciation. All of these lead up to a structured speaking task, in which students apply the skills and language they have developed over the course of the entire unit.

ON CAMPUS

PARTICIPATION AND CLASSROOM BEHAVIOR

PREPARING TO LISTEN

1 Work with a partner. Look at the pictures. Who looks interested? Who looks bored? How do you know?

LISTENING

2 ▶ 6.7 Listen to the conversation. Why is the teacher talking to Sam?

3 ▶ 6.7 Listen to the conversation again. Write *T* (true) or *F* (false)

_____ 1 Sam does not like the class.
_____ 2 The class is difficult.
_____ 3 Sam was tired in class today.
_____ 4 Sam often looks at his cell phone in class.
_____ 5 The teacher thinks that Sam does not pay attention.
_____ 6 Sam asks a lot of questions in class.

4 Work in small groups. Discuss the questions.

1 Why does the teacher think Sam is not paying attention?
2 What does the teacher want Sam to do?

Participation and classroom behavior
Instructors and professors in North America expect students to actively participate in class. Classroom participation is often part of your final grade.

146 UNIT 6

---

4 On Campus

Skills for college life

This unique section teaches students valuable skills beyond academic listening and speaking. From asking questions in class to participating in a study group and from being an active listener to finding help, students learn how to navigate university life. The section begins with a context-setting listening, and moves directly into active practice of the skill.

WHAT MAKES *PRISM* SPECIAL: CRITICAL THINKING

Bloom's Taxonomy

In order to truly prepare for college coursework, students need to develop a full range of thinking skills. *Prism* teaches explicit critical thinking skills in every unit of every level. These skills adhere to the taxonomy developed by Benjamin Bloom. By working within the taxonomy, we are able to ensure that your students learn both lower-order and higher-order thinking skills.

Critical thinking exercises are accompanied by icons indicating where the activities fall in Bloom's Taxonomy.

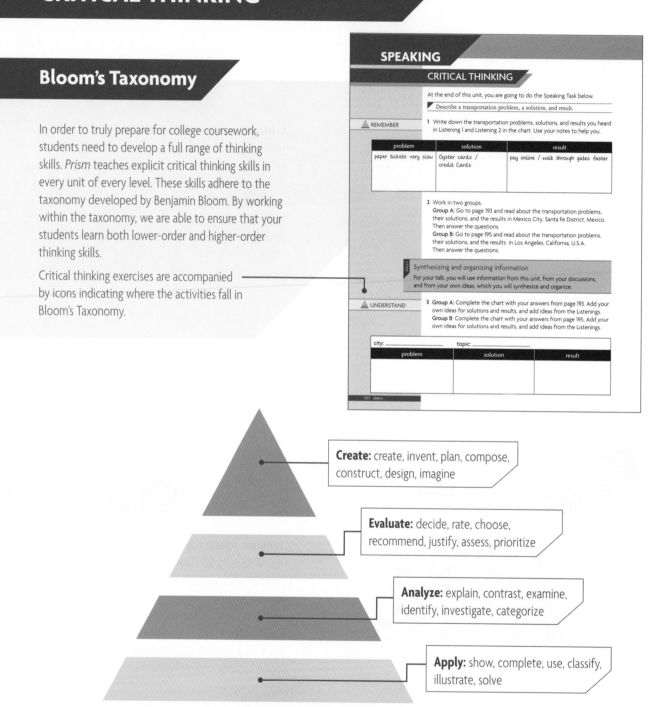

Create: create, invent, plan, compose, construct, design, imagine

Evaluate: decide, rate, choose, recommend, justify, assess, prioritize

Analyze: explain, contrast, examine, identify, investigate, categorize

Apply: show, complete, use, classify, illustrate, solve

Understand: compare, discuss, restate, predict, translate, outline

Remember: name, describe, relate, find, list, write, tell

WHAT MAKES *PRISM* SPECIAL: CRITICAL THINKING

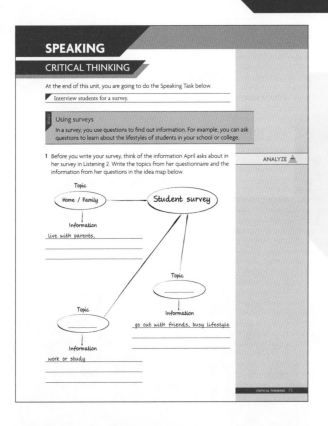

Higher-Order Thinking Skills

Create, **Evaluate**, and **Analyze** are critical skills for students in any college setting. Academic success depends on their abilities to derive knowledge from collected data, make educated judgments, and deliver insightful presentations. *Prism* helps students get there by creating activities such as categorizing information, comparing data, selecting the best solution to a problem, and developing arguments for a discussion or presentation.

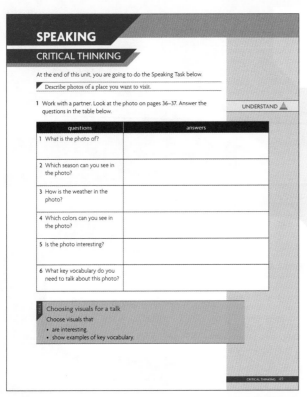

Lower-Order Thinking Skills

Apply, **Understand**, and **Remember** provide the foundation upon which all thinking occurs. Students need to be able to recall information, comprehend it, and see its use in new contexts. *Prism* develops these skills through exercises such as taking notes, mining notes for specific data, demonstrating comprehension, and distilling information from charts.

WHAT MAKES *PRISM* SPECIAL: ON CAMPUS

More college skills
Students need more than traditional academic skills. *Prism* teaches important skills for being engaged and successful all around campus, from emailing professors to navigating study groups.

Professors
Students learn how to take good lecture notes and how to communicate with professors and academic advisors.

Beyond the classroom
Skills include how to utilize campus resources, where to go for help, how to choose classes, and more.

Active learning
Students practice participating in class, in online discussion boards, and in study groups.

Texts
Learners become proficient at taking notes and annotating textbooks as well as conducting research online and in the library.

LISTENING 2

PREPARING TO LISTEN

1 You are going to listen to two students describe a landscape. Look at the photos of landscapes and answer the questions.

1 What season is it in each photo?
2 Describe the weather.
3 What colors can you see?

USING VISUALS TO PREDICT CONTENT

2 Match the words from the box to numbers 1–7 in the photos.

desert (n) a large, hot, dry area with very few plants _____
forest (n) a large area of trees growing closely together _____
island (n) an area of land that has water around it _____
mountain (n) a very high hill _____
park (n) a large area of grass and trees, usually very beautiful and everybody can use it _____
sea (n) a large area of salt water _____
sky (n) the area above the Earth where you can see clouds and the sun _____

UNDERSTANDING KEY VOCABULARY

PRISM Online Workbook

LISTENING 2 47

Vocabulary Research

Learning the right words

Students need to learn a wide range of general and academic vocabulary in order to be successful in college. *Prism* carefully selects the vocabulary that students study based on the General Service List, the Academic Word List, and the Cambridge English Corpus.

PRONUNCIATION FOR LISTENING

PRISM Online Workbook

Linking words

In English, you connect the end sound of a word with the beginning sound of the next word. This is called "linking words." Look at the how consonant sounds are linked to vowel sounds.

Sandy Singh lives_in_India.
Because_it's_a_good_idea.

3 6.1 Read the phrases from the interview. How do we pronounce the red and blue letters? Listen. Then circle the correct answer below.

1 an author of many books
2 I help architects.
3 For example
4 good ideas
5 restaurants in Los Angeles
6 What about the U.S.?

a We do not pronounce the red letters.
b We do not pronounce the blue letters.
c We pronounce the red and blue letters together.

WHILE LISTENING

GLOSSARY
architect (n) someone who designs buildings
design (n) the way something is planned and made
manage (v) to be responsible for an office, shop, people, etc.
psychologist (n) someone who knows about people's thoughts and feelings

LISTENING FOR MAIN IDEAS

4 6.2 Listen to an interview on the radio. Circle the correct answers.

1 Dr. Thompson is ...
   a a psychologist.
   b an architect.
   c a restaurant manager.

2 Many Mexican restaurants have ...
   a orange walls.
   b red walls.
   c white walls.

3 Many Chinese restaurants have ...
   a orange walls and floors.
   b red walls and floors.
   c white walls and floors.

4 The main topic of the interview is ...
   a older buildings.
   b colors and feelings.
   c good food in restaurants.

LISTENING 1 131

Pronunciation for Listening

Training your ears

This unique feature teaches learners to listen for specific features of spoken English that typically inhibit comprehension. Learners become primed to better understand detail and nuance while listening.

LEARNING OBJECTIVES

Listening skills	Understand key vocabulary; take notes
Pronunciation	Syllable stress
Speaking skill	Introduce and start a talk
Speaking Task	Talk about a famous person from your country
On Campus	Formal and informal language

ACTIVATE YOUR KNOWLEDGE

Work with a partner. Ask and answer the questions.

1 What can you see in the photo?
2 What is happening?
3 What do you think the people are saying?

WATCH AND LISTEN

PREPARING TO WATCH

ACTIVATING YOUR
KNOWLEDGE

1 Work with a partner and answer the questions.

1 Do most men and women work in your country?
2 Do men and women have the same or different jobs?
3 What do women in your country do in their free time? Do men have the same or different hobbies?
4 What jobs and hobbies do the women and men in your home have?

PREDICTING CONTENT
USING VISUALS

2 Look at the photos from the video. Circle the correct answer.

1 The woman is working in *an office / at home*.
2 The family is *happy / sad*.
3 The view of the *city / country* is interesting.
4 The man likes to *ride his bike / run*.

GLOSSARY

busy (adj) when you are busy, you have a lot of things to do

exercise (v) to do an activity, like running or swimming, to make your body strong

relax (v) to be calm and comfortable

schedule (n) a list of dates and times that shows when things happen

---

WHILE WATCHING

3 ▶ Watch the video. Write *T* (true) or *F* (false) next to the statements.

UNDERSTANDING MAIN IDEAS

_____ 1 Karen is not very busy.

_____ 2 Karen lives in an apartment.

_____ 3 Karen has four children.

_____ 4 Karen makes schedules for her children.

_____ 5 Scott is Karen's husband.

4 ▶ Watch again. Put the sentences in the correct order.

UNDERSTANDING DETAILS

1 Scott exercises every day. _____

2 Karen lives with her family in New York City. _____

3 Karen helps people make money. _____

4 Everyone is busy. _____

5 Her favorite room is the living room. _____

5 Match the two parts of the sentences.

MAKING INFERENCES

1 Karen likes   a a pet.

2 Karen's family lives in   b sports.

3 Karen's family has   c her job.

4 Karen's husband likes   d New York City and the country.

DISCUSSION

6 Work with a partner and answer the questions.

1 Do you have a busy job, or do you know anyone with a busy job? What job is it?

2 Which is better for you, an apartment in the city or a house in the country? Why?

3 Which sports do you like?

LISTENING

LISTENING 1

PREPARING TO LISTEN

USING YOUR
KNOWLEDGE

1 Talk with a partner. When you meet people for the first time, what do you tell them about yourself?

- your name?
- your last name?
- your family?
- your job?

Understanding key vocabulary

Before you listen, try to understand the key vocabulary in the Preparing to Listen exercises. These words will help you understand the main ideas of the listening.

UNDERSTANDING
KEY VOCABULARY

PRISM Online Workbook

2 You are going to listen to four students talk about themselves. Before you listen, read about two other students. Then write the words in bold from the texts in the chart below.

My name's Fahd, and I'm from Saudi Arabia. I'm 19, and I'm a **student**. I have a **brother** and three **sisters**. My **family**'s from Riyadh, but my brother has a house in Jeddah. He's a **doctor** there.

My name's Li Yu Lin, and I'm from China. I'm 21, and I'm a student. I have one brother. He is an **engineer**. We have a hotel in Shanghai. My **mother** and **father** are the **managers**.

topic	key vocabulary
family	brother, ...
jobs	student, ...

PRONUNCIATION FOR LISTENING

> **Syllable stress**
>
> When a word has more than one syllable, one syllable in the word has more stress than the others. You say it in a longer, louder way than the other syllables. The stressed syllables in these words are underlined.
>
> <u>bro</u>-ther   <u>man</u>-a-ger   <u>sis</u>-ter

3 ▶ 1.1 How many syllables do these words have? Listen and write *1, 2,* or *3* in the boxes.

1 introduce ☐
2 please ☐
3 Peru ☐

4 Turkey ☐
5 twenty ☐
6 eighteen ☐

7 study ☐
8 business ☐
9 computer ☐

10 college ☐

4 ▶ 1.1 Listen again. Underline the stressed syllables in Exercise 3.

PRISM **Online** Workbook

WHILE LISTENING

5 ▶ 1.2 Listen to four students. Match the countries to the people.

LISTENING FOR
MAIN IDEAS

Peru   Japan   Turkey   United Arab Emirates

1 Hussain _____

2 Nehir _____

3 Carlos _____

4 Koko _____

6 ▶ 1.2 Listen again. Circle the correct answers.

1 The students talk about
    a teachers in their school.   **c** their friends at home.
    b students in their class.

2 They tell us about their
    a families.   **b** vacations.   **c** homes.

3 They also tell us what they want to
    a do on vacation.   **b** do at home.   **c** study in college.

7 ▶ 1.2 Write *T* (true) or *F* (false) next to the sentences. Then listen again and check your answers.

_____ 1 Koko is 18.   _____ 4 Nehir is 19.
_____ 2 Koko's a student.   _____ 5 Nehir has a sister.
_____ 3 Hussain is from Turkey.   _____ 6 Carlos wants to study business.

8 Work with a partner. Ask and answer questions about the students in Exercise 5. Take notes in the chart.

1 What's his / her name?
2 How old is he / she?
3 Where's he / she from?
4 Does he / she have any brothers or sisters?
5 What does he / she want to do in the future?

	1 What's his / her name?	2 How old is he / she?	3 Where's he / she from?	4 Does he / she have any brothers or sisters?	5 What does he / she want to do in the future?
student 1	Koko				
student 2					
student 3					
student 4					

DISCUSSION

9 Work with a partner. Talk about the things below:

- your name (*I'm ...*).
- what you do (*I'm ...*).
- your country and hometown (*I'm from ...*).
- people in your family (*I have ...* , *My father's a ...* , *My mother's a ...*).
- your plans for the future (*I want to ...*).

10 Work with a new partner. Talk about your partner in Exercise 9.

This is [Paolo]. He's / She's [18]. He's / She's from [Brazil]. He's / She's a [student]. He's / She's from [Recife]. He / She has [two sisters]. He / She wants to [study business].

SUBJECT PRONOUNS AND POSSESSIVE ADJECTIVES

subject pronouns	possessive adjectives
I	my
you	your
he	his
she	her
it	its
we	our
they	their

Use subject pronouns before a verb.

I(m) Carlos.

She(s) a student in our class.

He (wants) to study business.

Use possessive adjectives before a noun.

My family's from Bogotá.

Her mother's from Sapporo.

His father's from Al-Ain.

PRISM Online Workbook

1 Look at the underlined word(s). Write the correct subject pronouns in the blanks to replace the underlined words.

1 <u>My sister</u> is a doctor. _____ works in a hospital

2 <u>My parents</u> work in a hotel. _____ 're managers.

3 <u>My</u> name is Koko. _____ 'm a student.

4 Where is <u>Recife</u>? _____ 's in Brazil.

5 <u>Reina and Mari</u> are both from Canada. _____ 're from Toronto.

6 <u>My brother and I</u> are students. _____ 're in two classes together.

2 Write the correct possessive adjectives in the blanks.

1 This is Koko's book. → This is _____her_____ book.

2 This is my brother's car. → This is _____ car.

3 This is our daughter's school. → This is _____ school.

4 This is Pedro and Isobel's house. → This is _____ house.

5 This is my town and my family's town. → This is _____ town.

3 Circle the correct answers.

1 *She / Her* name's Kerry.
2 Is this *you / your* house?
3 This bag is nice. Is it *you / your* bag?
4 *He / His* is the manager of a shop.
5 *They / Their* teacher is from Egypt.

6 I'd like to study at this college. *It / Its* courses are very good.
7 *I / My* have a problem with *I / my* computer.
8 *We / Our* have a restaurant in *we / our* hotel.

THE VERB *BE*

LANGUAGE

subject	*be*	
I	*am*	
You / We / They	*are*	from Toronto.
He / She / It	*is*	

Contractions:	
singular	**plural**
I am → I'm	We **are** → We're
You **are** → You're	You **are** → You're
He **is** / She **is** / It **is** → He's / She's / It's	They **are** → They're

In conversation, it is normal to use contractions.

I'm from the U.S.   **It's** a photo of my friend.   **They're** from Toronto.

Add *not* to make the negative.

singular			plural		
subject	*be+not*		subject	*be+not*	
I	am **not**		You		
You	are **not**	a student.	We	are **not**	Canadian.
He / She / It	is **not**		They		

negative contractions	
singular	**plural**
I am not → I'm **not**	You are not → You're **not** / You **aren't**
You are not → You're **not** / You **aren't**	We are not → We're **not** / We **aren't**
He is not → He's **not** / He **isn't**	They are not → They're **not** / They **aren't**
She is not → She's **not** / She **isn't**	
It is not → It's **not** / It **isn't**	

The verb is before the subject in questions.

What's her name? **Is** she from Turkey? **Are** you from New York?

4 ▶ 1.3 Listen and circle the forms you hear.

A

Kerry: (1) *Who's / Who is* your best friend, Yasemin?

Yasemin: Her (2) *name's / name is* Meral.

Kerry: How (3) *old is / old's* she?

Yasemin: She's 20.

Kerry: Is she from Turkey?

Yasemin: Yes, but she (4) *is not / isn't* from Ankara like me. (5) *She is / She's* from Izmir.

B

Ryo: Excuse me, Kerry. Are you from Toronto?

Kerry: No, no, (6) *I am not / I'm not* from Canada. (7) *I am / I'm* from the United States. But my grandparents are Canadian. They (8) *are not / 're not* from Toronto. (9) *They are / They're* from Montreal.

Ryo: Are your parents American?

Kerry: Yes—and my sisters. (10) *We are / We're* all American.

5 Complete the dialogue with the correct form of *be*. Add *not* if necessary.

A: (1) _____Is_____ your school in Cairo?

B: No, it (2) _____ . It (3) _____ in Abu Dhabi in the UAE.

A: (4) _____ you from there?

B: Yes, I (5) _____ .

A: What do you study?

B: Business.

A: (6) _____ your parents in business?

B: No, they (7) _____ . My mother (8) _____ a doctor, and my father (9) _____ a teacher.

A: Do you have brothers and sisters?

B: Yes, I have two brothers.

A: (10) _____ they students?

B: Yes. We (11) _____ all students at the same college.

6 Work with a partner. Practice the dialogue. Give answers that are true for you.

PREPARING TO LISTEN

1 What do you think is the best job in the world? What do you think is the worst? Compare with a partner. Does he or she agree?

2 You are going to listen to two students talk about a famous person (someone many people know) from their country. Look at the photos. What are the people's jobs? Use the jobs in the vocabulary box to help you. More than one job is possible.

USING YOUR KNOWLEDGE

UNDERSTANDING KEY VOCABULARY

> **businessman** (n)   **businesswoman** (n)
> **chef** (n)   **scientist** (n)   **teacher** (n)   **writer** (n)

a Alice Waters knows about food.

_____

b Salman Khan—Education for all

_____

c Larry Page—Co-founder of Google

_____

d Ursula Burns—CEO of Xerox

_____

e Bil Nye—The Science Guy

_____

f Mario Batali cooking

_____

3 Work with a partner. Answer the questions. Which of the jobs from Exercise 2 would you like to do? Why?

4 ▶ 1.4 Listen to the words for jobs in Exercise 2. Write the number of syllables in each word next to it. Then listen again and underline the stressed syllables.

1 writer _____

2 teacher _____

3 businessman _____

4 businesswoman _____

5 chef _____

6 scientist _____

LISTENING FOR
MAIN IDEAS

WHILE LISTENING

> **GLOSSARY**
>
> **creative** (adj) good at thinking of new ideas or using imagination
>
> **free** (adj) not costing any money
>
> **healthy** (adj) good for your health
>
> **owner** (n) a person who owns something

5 ▶ 1.5 Listen to two students, Marie and Clare, talk about two famous people from their country. The people are in the photos in Exercise 2. Answer the questions.

1 Which person does Marie talk about? _____

2 What job does Marie's person have? _____

3 Which person does Clare talk about? _____

4 What job does Clare's person have? _____

SKILLS

Taking notes

When you listen to a talk or a conversation, it's a good idea to take notes. When you take notes, you write down the important information you hear. You do not need to write complete sentences.

6 ▶ 1.5 Listen again and take notes.

Alice Waters:	family	_____
	famous for	_____
	other information	_____
Salman Khan:	family	_____
	famous for	_____
	other information	_____

7 ▶ 1.5 Match the start of the sentences with the endings. Use your notes from Exercise 6 to help you. Then listen again and check your answers.

1 Alice's husband is
2 Both Alice and Salman are
3 Alice is a writer
4 Salman's mother is
5 Salman has
6 Alice's family is
7 Salman is
8 Salman's wife is

a from the U.S.
b a doctor.
c a businessman.
d very creative.
e and a chef.
f from India.
g a son and daughter.
h from California.

DISCUSSION

8 Work with a partner.

Student A: Go to page 192.
Student B: Go to page 194.

SPEAKING

CRITICAL THINKING

At the end of this unit, you are going to do the Speaking Task below.

> Tell your group about a famous person from your country.

SKILLS

Using idea maps

An *idea map* helps you think about the topic and organize information about it. It also helps you to remember key information and vocabulary.

ANALYZE

1 Look at the idea map below and answer the questions.

   1 What is the main topic of the map?

   2 What are the three other topics in the map?

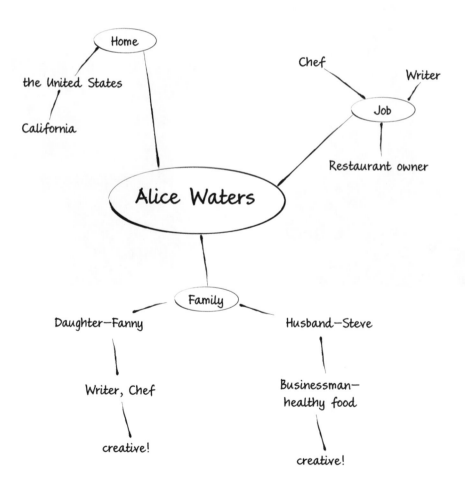

2 Write information about Salman Khan in the idea map. Use your notes from Listening 2 to help you. Add more circles and lines for your information.

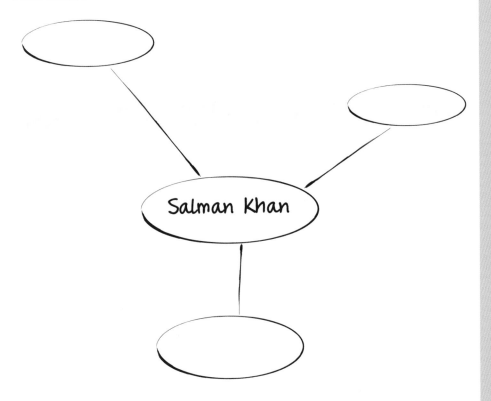

3 Make an idea map for a famous person from your country.

1 Think of a famous person from your country.
2 Write the name of the person in the center.
3 Find a photo and information about the person on the Internet.
4 Think about the person's country, job, family, home and why they are famous. Write key words for these topics (for example, husband—Steve, restaurant owner, 1 daughter, creative family). Add them to your idea map.

4 Work with a partner. Ask and answer questions about the people in your idea map.

- Who's the person in your idea map?
- Who's in his / her family?
- Where's he / she from?
- What is his / her job?
- Why is he / she famous?

COUNTRIES AND NATIONALITIES

1 Work with a partner. Complete the table with words for nationalities.

Student A: Go to page 192.
Student B: Go to page 194.

name	country	nationality
Ana García	Mexico	(1)
Eunseong Kim	South Korea	(2)
Karim Abdel Aziz	Egypt	(3)
Lin Dan	China	Chinese
Majid Al Futtaim	UAE	(4)
Haruki Murakami	Japan	(5)
Zeynep Ahunbay	Turkey	(6)
Sebastião Salgado	Brazil	(7)
Shakira	Colombia	(8)

2 Write words from the table in the blanks.

1 Eunseong Kim is a famous _____ scientist.
2 Ana García is from _____ .
3 Karim Abdel Aziz is an _____ actor.
4 Haruki Murakami is from _____ .
5 Lin Dan is a famous _____ badminton player.
6 Sebastião Salgado is a famous _____ photographer.
7 Shakira's a famous singer from _____ .
8 Majid Al Futtaim is a famous _____ businessman.

VOCABULARY FOR JOBS

3 Look at the words for jobs. Add other job words from this unit to the chart.

word + *er / r*	writer
word + *or*	act*or*
word + *ist*	journal*ist*
other forms	chef

INTRODUCING AND STARTING A TALK

4 1.6 Circle the correct phrases. Then listen and check.

1 _____ about a famous person from Mexico.
   a I'm going to tell for you
   b I'm going to tell you
   c I'm going to tell
2 Ana García is _____ .
   a famous Mexican chef
   b a famous Mexican chef
   c the famous Mexican chef
3 _____ Haruki Murakami.
   a It has
   b This has
   c This is
4 _____ a famous Japanese writer.
   a His is
   b It is
   c He's

PRONUNCIATION FOR SPEAKING

SKILLS

Word stress in sentences

You stress important words in sentences. Important words are usually nouns, verbs, and adjectives. You say the words more strongly than the other words. The words that are less important are said more weakly.

<u>Ana García</u> is from <u>Mexico</u>.

She's a <u>famous</u> <u>chef</u>.

I'm going to <u>tell</u> you about a <u>famous</u> person from <u>Egypt</u>.

PRISM Online Workbook

5 ▶ 1.7 Listen, read, and repeat.

1 Karim Abdel Aziz is a famous actor.
2 Karim's father is Mohammed Abdel Aziz.
3 He's a film director.
4 Karim's aunt is Samira Muhsin.
5 She's an actor.

6 ▶ 1.7 Underline the stressed words in the sentences in Exercise 5. Then listen and repeat again.

7 Work with a partner. Write *noun*, *verb*, or *adjective* next to your underlined words.

8 Change the sentences so they are true about people from your country.

I'm going to <u>tell</u> you about a <u>famous person</u> from China.
<u>Lin Dan</u>'s a <u>famous badminton</u> player.

9 Practice saying your sentences.

SPEAKING TASK

> Tell your group about a famous person from your country.

PREPARE

1 Look back at your idea map in Critical Thinking. Review your notes and add any new information you want to include in your presentation. In your talk you will:

- Introduce your person.
- Show your photo.
- Talk about your person's job, family, and home. Talk about why your person is famous.

2 Prepare an introduction for your talk.

3 Refer to the Task Checklist as you prepare your talk.

TASK CHECKLIST	✔
Use an idea map.	
Talk about a famous person from your country.	
Use the verb *be*, possessive adjectives, and subject pronouns correctly.	
Use sentence stress correctly.	

PRACTICE

4 Practice giving your talk with a partner. Listen to your partner's talk and ask questions.

PRESENT

5 Work in small groups. Talk about the famous person from your country. Show people in your group your photo. When you listen to other students, take notes in the chart about each person.

	person 1	person 2	person 3	person 4
name				
country				
job				
family				
home				
famous				

6 Talk in your group. Which person would you like to meet? Why? Tell the class.

ON CAMPUS

FORMAL AND INFORMAL LANGUAGE

PREPARING TO LISTEN

1 You are going to listen to people meeting for the first time. Look at the pictures. What do you think they are saying?

WHILE LISTENING

2 ▶ 1.8 Listen to two conversations. Circle the topics you hear.

> the syllabus   Paris   the class website   homework   coffee

---

SKILLS

Formal and informal language

When you speak to a teacher or a professor, use formal language. You can use informal language with your friends and classmates.

---

3 ▶ 1.8 Look at the phrases from the listening. Check (✔) conversation A or conversation B. Then listen again and check your answers.

	conversation A	conversation B
1 My name is Carlos Mendoza.		
2 Hi, how are you doing?		
3 Hey ... can I borrow a pen?		
4 I'm sorry I'm late.		
5 Is it possible to have some information about the class?		
6 Yes, of course.		
7 Sure. Here you go.		
8 Thank you very much, professor.		
9 Thanks a lot.		
10 I'm Tony.		

PRACTICE

4 Decide which phrases in Exercise 3 are more formal and which are more informal.

5 Write examples from Exercise 3 on the lines below.

More formal	More informal
1 _____	I'm Tony.
Good morning / afternoon / evening.	Hi.
How are you?	**3** _____
May I ... ? Is it possible to ... ?	Can I ... ?
Of course.	**4** _____
2 _____	Thanks a lot.
Goodbye.	Bye. / See you later.
Yes.	Yeah.

6 Work with a partner. Student A is a professor. Student B is a student. Write possible answers to the questions below.

Professor	Student
1 What is your name?	_____
2 How can I help you?	_____
3 Do you have any questions?	_____
4 I'll see you on Thursday?	_____

7 Work with a partner. You are both students. Write answers to the questions and phrases below.

Student A	Student B
1 How are you doing?	_____
2 Can I borrow a pen?	_____
3 Hi. I'm Sam.	_____
4 Where are you from?	_____
5 Nice to meet you.	_____

8 Practice the conversations.

REAL-WORLD APPLICATION

9 Work with a partner. Choose one of the situations and role-play it.

You are in a classroom. You are a new student. Ask your teacher for some information about the class textbook.

You are in a classroom. Ask your professor for an appointment to discuss a problem with the homework.

You are in a classroom. Introduce yourself to another student and have a short conversation. Finish the conversation by saying *It was nice to meet you.*

LEARNING OBJECTIVES

Listening skill	Use visuals to predict content
Pronunciation	Sentence stress
Speaking skills	Give a talk; describe photos; adjectives
Speaking Task	Describe photos of a place you want to visit
On Campus	Asking for clarification

ACTIVATE YOUR KNOWLEDGE

Work with a partner. Ask and answer the questions.

1 What do you see in the photo?

2 What is unusual about this photo?

3 Do you like hot or cold weather?

WATCH AND LISTEN

PREPARING TO WATCH

ACTIVATING YOUR KNOWLEDGE

1 Work with a partner. Discuss the questions.

1 How many seasons are there in your country?
2 Does it rain often? When?
3 What are the most famous deserts in the world?
4 What is the weather in a desert like?

PREDICTING CONTENT USING VISUALS

2 Look at the pictures from the video. Write *T* (true) or *F* (false) next to the statements.

_____ 1 A desert is dry.
_____ 2 It does not rain often in a desert.
_____ 3 There are several deserts on Earth.
_____ 4 A desert is flat.

> **GLOSSARY**
>
> **climate** (n) the weather of a particular place
> **equator** (n) an imaginary line around the center of the Earth
> **inch** (n) a unit of measure, about 2.5 centimeters
> **spin** (v) to turn around and around

WHILE WATCHING

UNDERSTANDING MAIN IDEAS

3 ▶ Watch the video. Circle the correct answer.

1 A desert is *very hot / not very hot* in the summer during the day.
2 A desert *has / does not have* a lot of water.
3 *There are / there are not* different plants in a desert.
4 Hot air comes from *the equator / the desert*.

4 ▶ Watch again. Circle the correct answers.

1 The Sonoran Desert is in _____ .
   a North Africa
   b the Middle East
   c North America
2 In the summer, the temperature in the Sonoran Desert can reach _____ .
   a 122° F (50° C)
   b 22° F (-5° C)
   c 112° F (44° C)
3 There are more deserts like the Sonoran desert in _____ .
   a South America, Japan, and North Africa
   b the Middle East, India, and North Africa
   c Taiwan, India, and North Africa

5 Write the words from the box in the blanks.

| careful   difficult   fruits and vegetables   rain |

1 It is _____ to live in a desert.
2 There is little _____ in a desert.
3 Many _____ do not grow in a desert.
4 People need to be _____ in a desert.

DISCUSSION

6 Work with a partner. Discuss the questions.

1 Is there a desert in your country? What is the desert's name?
2 How is the climate different in a desert?
3 Would you like to live in or near a desert? Why or why not?

LISTENING

LISTENING 1

PREPARING TO LISTEN

1 You are going to listen to a talk about different seasons. Use the words in the box to complete the sentences.

> **cold** (adj) having a low temperature
> **fall** (n) the season of the year between summer and winter
> **hot** (adj) having a high temperature
> **snow** (n) soft, white pieces of frozen water that fall from the sky
> **spring** (n) the season of the year between winter and summer
> **temperature** (n) how hot or cold something is
> **weather** (n) the temperature or conditions outside, for example, if it is hot, cold, sunny, etc.

1 The sun is very _____ .
2 Brrr! I'm _____ . I need my hat and jacket.
3 The _____ is beautiful! It's white and clean. This is my favorite kind of _____ .
4 _____ is between winter and summer.
5 It's _____ now. The trees are red and orange, and it's almost winter.
6 The _____ is -30 Fahrenheit (-34.4 Celsius). Let's stay inside.

2 Work with a partner. Discuss your answers.

Describe the weather in your country.
What is your favorite season? Use the words in the box above to help you.

Using visuals to predict content

Visuals can be photos, pictures, graphs, or tables. Use visuals to help you understand the topic and important ideas.

3 Look at the photos and answer the questions.

1 These photos are all from the same place. Would you like to visit this place? Why or why not?
2 Which photo has hot weather? _____
3 Which photo has a beach (an area next to water with sand or small stones where people like to sit)? _____
4 Which photo has cold weather? _____
5 What season can you see in each photo? _____
6 What's the temperature outside in each photo? _____

PRONUNCIATION FOR LISTENING

Sentence stress

We stress important words in a sentence. Important words can be:

- <u>nouns</u>: *Dubai, July, Canada, lot, snow, winter, places*
- (adjectives) *hot, sunny, cold*
- verbs: (but not *be*): *has, get*

<u>Dubai</u>'s (hot) in <u>July</u>.
<u>Canada</u> has a <u>lot</u> of <u>snow</u> in <u>winter</u>.
We get <u>snow</u> when it's (cold) here.

PRISM Online Workbook

4 ▶ 2.1 Listen to the sentences and

- underline the nouns.
- circle the adjectives.
- highlight the verbs (but not *be*).

1 Take a look at the photos.
2 They are all from one place.
3 There's a beautiful beach next to a big lake.
4 It's winter, and there's a mountain.
5 It's hot, and there's sand.

WHILE LISTENING

LISTENING FOR
MAIN IDEAS

5 ▶ 2.2 Listen to a talk about a place with four seasons. Which photos does the teacher talk about?

LISTENING FOR DETAILS

6 ▶ 2.2 Listen again. Complete the sentences with the missing words.

1 It's a _____ day in summer.
2 There's lots of _____ and a forest.
3 It's also very _____ .
4 You can see it's _____ .
5 The temperature is a little cold, and the trees change color to _____ and _____ .
6 After the cold weather, _____ is welcome in Minnesota.
7 The weather is warm and it _____ , so the flowers grow.

7 ▶ 2.2 Listen again and check your answers.

DISCUSSION

8 Work in groups.

1 Choose a photo, but do not say which one.
2 Take turns talking about your photo. Use the phrases from the box.
3 Listen to the other students and guess the photo.

> Take a look at this photo. What can we see?
> It's ... hot, cold.
> This season is ... summer, winter, fall, spring.
> There's a ... beach, lake.
> There's ... snow.

SEASONS

PRISM Online Workbook

1 ▶ 2.3 Listen and match the words for seasons to the correct sentences.

1 spring
2 summer
3 fall
4 winter
5 the dry season
6 the rainy season

a Canada gets a lot of snow in _____ .
b _____ in Washington, D.C., begins in June. It gets very hot.
c _____ in New York is from March to May. There are a lot of beautiful flowers.
d In _____ , the trees change color from green to orange or red.
e In Korea, Japan, and China, _____ begins in June and ends in July. It gets very wet.
f _____ in Brazil begins in May. There is not a lot of rain.

WEATHER

PRISM Online Workbook

2 Match the pictures to the words for weather.

picture	noun	adjective
	sun	sunny
	snow	snowy
	wind	windy
	rain	rainy
	cloud	cloudy
	storm	stormy

3 Circle the correct word.

1 I'm happy when it's *sun / sunny*.
2 There's a big, black *cloud / cloudy* in the sky.
3 I have a hat for when it's *rain / rainy*.
4 We get a lot of *storms / stormy* in April.

COLORS

4 Match the words from the box to the correct color.

red _____   black _____
blue _____   white _____
yellow _____   orange _____
green _____

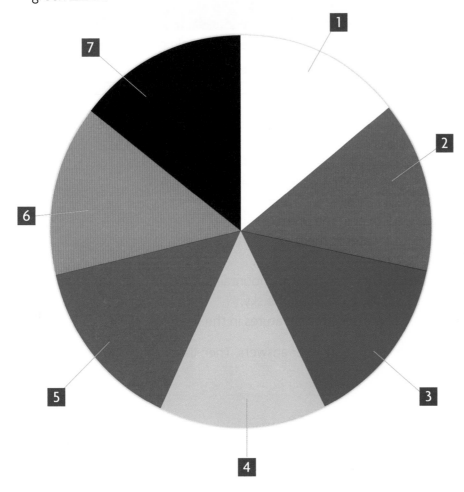

5 Work with a partner. Ask and answer the questions from the box about the words and phrases below.

> What color is ... ?   It's ... / It can be ... or ...
> What color are ... ?   They're ... / They can be ... or ...

1 water   4 sand
2 snow   5 clouds
3 trees   6 your family's car

THERE IS ... / THERE ARE ...

There is ... / There are ...

You can use *There is ...* (*There's ...*) / *There are ...* to talk about new information, people, places, and things.

Singular	Plural
There is snow. / **There's** snow.	**There are** people on the beach.
	There are rivers.

PRISM Online Workbook

6 Complete the sentences below with the phrases from the box. Use the nouns to help you.

> There's a   There's   There are

1 _____ river in the photo.
2 _____ water in the lake.
3 _____ stones on the beach.
4 _____ small town in the mountains.
5 _____ black clouds in the sky.
6 _____ extreme temperatures in the winter.

7 ▶ 2.4 Listen and check your answers. Then listen again and repeat.

LISTENING 2

PREPARING TO LISTEN

1 You are going to listen to two students describe a landscape. Look at the photos of landscapes and answer the questions.

USING VISUALS TO PREDICT CONTENT

1 What season is it in each photo?
2 Describe the weather.
3 What colors can you see?

2 Match the words from the box to numbers 1–7 in the photos.

UNDERSTANDING KEY VOCABULARY

PRISM Online Workbook

> **desert** (n) a large, hot, dry area with very few plants _____
> **forest** (n) a large area of trees growing closely together _____
> **island** (n) an area of land that has water around it _____
> **mountain** (n) a very high hill _____
> **park** (n) a large area of grass and trees, usually very beautiful and everybody can use it _____
> **sea** (n) a large area of salt water _____
> **sky** (n) the area above the Earth where you can see clouds and the sun _____

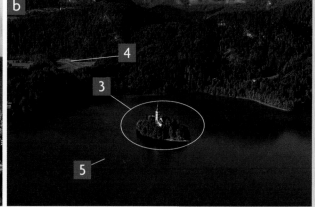

WHILE LISTENING

3 ▶ 2.5 Listen to two students, Daniela and Altan, describe one of the landscapes from Exercise 2.

1 Which photo does Daniela describe? _____
2 Which photo does Altan describe? _____
3 Which photo do they not describe? _____

4 ▶ 2.5 Listen again and circle the correct answers.

1 Daniela describes a landscape
   a in *spring / summer*.
   b in *Italy / Turkey*.
   c with a *forest / beach*.
   d she thinks is *beautiful / snowy*.
2 Altan describes a landscape
   a in *his / another* country.
   b in *fall / winter*.
   c on a *hot / cold* day.
   d with a famous *park / hill*.

DISCUSSION

5 Think of Listening 1 and Listening 2 and discuss the questions with a partner.

1 Daniela describes a landscape. Which season does it match in Listening 1? How is it the same? How is it different?
2 Altan describes a landscape. Which season does it match in Listening 1? How is it the same? How is it different?
3 Do any seasons in your country have extreme temperatures? Which ones?

SPEAKING

CRITICAL THINKING

At the end of this unit, you are going to do the Speaking Task below.

Describe photos of a place you want to visit.

1 Work with a partner. Look at the photo on pages 36–37. Answer the questions in the table below.

Look at the photo on pages 36–37.

UNDERSTAND ▲

questions	answers
1 What is the photo of?	
2 Which season can you see in the photo?	
3 How is the weather in the photo?	
4 Which colors can you see in the photo?	
5 Is the photo interesting?	
6 What key vocabulary do you need to talk about this photo?	

SKILLS

Choosing visuals for a talk

Choose visuals that

- are interesting.
- show examples of key vocabulary.

2 Use an Internet search to find two photos of a place you would like to visit. First answer the questions.

1 What place would you like to visit? (e.g., New York, the Sahara Desert, Italy)
2 What seasons do you want in the photos? (e.g., summer, winter, the rainy season).

3 Use your answers from Exercise 2 in an Internet search. Use questions 1–6 in Exercise 1 to help you choose two good photos.

4 Answer questions 1–6 in Exercise 1 for the photos you found. Take notes.

5 Work with a partner. Take turns asking and answering the questions about your partner's photos. Use the phrases from the box to answer.

1 Where is it?
2 What season is it?
3 How is the weather?
4 What can you see there?

> It's in _____ . (country)
> It's _____ . (season)
> It's _____ . (weather adjective)
> You can see _____ . (place)
> There's a / There's _____ . (noun)
> There are _____ . (noun)

PREPARATION FOR SPEAKING

GIVING A TALK

PRISM Online Workbook

1 ▶ 2.6 Listen and match the two parts of the sentences.

a Good morning,   my first photo.
b I'm going to talk about   everybody.
c OK, so here's   photo of the park.
d Hello, everybody!   I'm Altan.
e I'm from   two photos of a place in spring.
f Here's my   first photo.
g Here's another   Samsun. Samsun is in Turkey.

PRONUNCIATION FOR SPEAKING

Sentence stress

In a normal sentence, one or two words have more stress than the others.
You say them in a longer, louder way than the other words.

2 ▶ 2.6 Listen again. Underline the words with stress in Exercise 1.

3 ▶ 2.6 Listen again and repeat. Say the underlined words louder.

DESCRIBING PHOTOS

4 Look at the photos. What can you see?

PRISM **Online** Workbook

5 ▶ 2.7 Match the phrases and sentences to make a talk. Then listen and check.

1 Hello, everybody!
2 Today
3 Here's my first photo.
4 OK, so where is this place?
5 Here's another photo of the mountain.
6 It's a beautiful place.

a It's in Japan. This is Mount Fuji.
b There's a path, and you can see there are people there. There are a lot of white clouds below.
c I'm going to talk about two photos of a place in spring.
d I want to go there.
e You can see there's a big mountain. There's a lot of snow. And there are trees. The trees are orange and red.
f OK, so I'm Khaled. I'm from Port Said.

6 Work with a partner. Take turns describing the photos. Look at the text in Exercise 5. Make Khaled's talk true for you.

Hello everybody! OK, so, I'm ~~Khaled~~ Laura.
I'm from ~~Port Said~~ Venezuela.

ADJECTIVES

Use adjectives to describe age (*young, old*), size (*big, small*), nationality (*Turkish, Brazilian*), color (*red, green*), and quality (*hot, cold*).

Adjectives go after the verb *be* (*am / is / are*) or before a noun.

The mountains ⟨are⟩ **tall**.
I⟨'m⟩ **Turkish**. The weather ⟨is⟩ **cold**. It⟨'s⟩ **windy**.
It's a **beautiful** place. It's a **sunny** day.
There are **white** clouds in the sky.

You often stress adjectives.

7 Choose the correct adjective for each sentence. Then add the adjective in the correct place in the sentence.

| beautiful   big   happy   orange and red   snowy   ~~white~~ |

1 There are clouds in the sky. ___white___
2 It's a day in winter. _____
3 There's a mountain. _____
4 The people are swimming. _____
5 There are trees. _____
6 It's a beach. _____

8 Correct the mistakes in the sentences.

1 It's sun in the photo.

_____

2 There's a windy.

_____

3 There's a mountain big.

_____

4 The people happy.

_____

5 There's a forest green.

_____

6 It's a rain day.

_____

Describe photos of a place you want to visit.

PREPARE

1 Look back at your notes in Critical Thinking. Review your notes and think of words and phrases to use in your talk. Write them down to help you with your talk.

2 Refer to the Task Checklist below as you prepare your talk.

TASK CHECKLIST	✔
Prepare an introduction.	
Find key vocabulary for the photos (what you can see in the photos, weather, season, etc.).	
Describe the photos of a place you want to visit.	
Use stress correctly in your sentences.	

3 Think of questions you can ask the other students using language you have seen in this unit.

> Can you see ... ?   Where is ... ?   What ... ?

PRACTICE

4 Practice your talk with a partner.

PRESENT

5 Work in groups.

1 Take turns describing photos or pictures of a place you want to visit.
2 Listen to the other students in your group. Take notes in the table and ask questions.

	example	student 1	student 2
student's name	Khaled		
country	Japan		
place	mountain		
season	spring		
weather	sunny		
things in the photos	There is a mountain. There are trees. There are clouds.		

ON CAMPUS

ASKING FOR CLARIFICATION

PREPARING TO LISTEN

1 You are going to listen to two students meeting for the first time. Look at the pictures and answer the questions.

    1 What can you see in the photo? Would you like to study there?

    2 Who do you ask for help when you start doing something new?

    3 Imagine it is your first week at this university. What questions do you have?

a university campus

WHILE LISTENING

2 ▶ 2.8 Listen to the conversation and circle the correct answer.

    1 Lixin (Lee) is
      a a first-year student.   **b** a second-year student.

    2 Maya is
      a beginning college.   **b** in the last year of college.

    3 Lee is going to meet with
      a her friend.   **b** her advisor.

    4 Lee is living
      a at home.   **b** on campus.

    5 Lee's roommate is from
      a China.   **b** Brazil.

    6 "RA" means
      a resident advisor.   **b** room assistant.

3 ▶ 2.8 Listen again. Write the correct word from the box in each sentence.

advisor   freshman   resident advisor   roommate   senior

    1 A first year student is a _____ .

    2 A student in the last year of college is a _____ .

    3 A(n) _____ lives with you in your dorm or apartment.

    4 A(n) _____ helps you choose your classes.

    5 A(n) _____ works in the dorm.

Asking for clarification and checking understanding

When you hear new information, it is sometimes difficult to understand it the first time you hear it. Use these expressions to ask for clarification or to hear the information again.

What is the word again?   I'm sorry. I don't understand.

How do you spell that?   Can you say that again, please?

Use these expressions to check understanding

Is that right?   Did you say ... ?

PRACTICE

4 Work with a partner. Look at the information on the card. Take turns asking and answering questions about the information. Ask for clarification or check understanding.

A *What is the student's name?*
B *Alex Vargas*
A *Did you say Vargas?*
B *And what's his ID number?*
A *It's ...*
B *Can you say that again, please?*

> **Student Name:** Alex Vargas
> **Student ID #:** Y23409960
> **Academic Advisor:** Prof. Carla Young   **Office:** 305
> **Advising meeting:** Wednesday, September 17, 2 pm
> **Dormitory:** Hiller Hall   **Resident Advisor:** Frank Chiu

REAL-WORLD APPLICATION

5 **Student A:** Look at the information card. You are the student. Write your name on the card and ask Student B questions to complete the information.

A What's my ID number?
B It's Y23 ...
A And who is my advisor?
A Can you spell that?

Student B: Go to page 194. Give the information to student A.

Now change roles.

Student A: Go to page 192 and give the information to Student B.

Student B: Complete the card and ask Student A for information and clarification and check understanding.

> **Student Name:** (Write your name here.)
> _____
> **Student ID #:** _____
> **Academic Advisor:** _____
> **Office:** _____
> **Advising meeting:** Date: _____
>   Time: _____
> **Dormitory:** _____
> **Resident Advisor:** _____

ACTIVATE YOUR KNOWLEDGE

1 What can you see in the photograph?

2 Why is the woman doing two things at the same time?

3 Circle the phrases that are true for you.

- use the Internet or a cell phone every day
- talk to friends every day
- do two things at the same time every day

WATCH AND LISTEN

PREPARING TO WATCH

ACTIVATING YOUR KNOWLEDGE

1 Read the sentences. Put a check (✔) next to the ones that are true for you.

- I have a busy lifestyle.
- I enjoy riding a bicycle.
- I like to go out with friends.
- I exercise regularly.

2 Work with a partner. Compare your answers from Exercise 1 and answer the questions.

1 How are you the same?
2 How are you different?

PREDICTING CONTENT USING VISUALS

3 Look at the photos from the video. Put the words in order to make sentences.

1 has / The town / a main street / .
2 active / people / are / The / .
3 Exercising / for / is important / many people / .

GLOSSARY

active (adj) doing a lot of things, or moving around a lot

focus (n) the person or thing that you are paying the most attention to

stationary bike (n) a machine that looks like a bicycle but does not move. You ride on it for exercise

weights (n) heavy pieces of metal that you lift up and down to make your body strong

WHILE WATCHING

4 ▶ Watch the video. Circle the correct answers.

1 Most of the people in The Villages *work / don't work* anymore.
2 The people in The Villages are happy and *active / lazy*.
3 The Villages is a place for people to *rest / stay active*.
4 There are *many / few* activities for people in The Villages.

UNDERSTANDING MAIN IDEAS

5 ▶ Watch again. Circle the correct answers.

1 More than _____ people live in The Villages.
   a 5,000   **b** 50,000   **c** 15,000
2 Americans are now living _____ years or more after they finish working.
   a 30   **b** 43   **c** 13
3 In the gym at The Villages, people _____ .
   a lift weights   **b** play golf   **c** go shopping

UNDERSTANDING DETAILS

6 Write *T* (true) or *F* (false) next to the statements.

_____ 1 People in The Villages like to try new activities.
_____ 2 The Villages is a good place to live if you like winter sports.
_____ 3 A healthy lifestyle is important for people in The Villages.
_____ 4 People who live in The Villages are from many different places.

MAKING INFERENCES

DISCUSSION

7 Work with a partner and answer the questions.

1 Would you like to live in The Villages? Why or why not?
2 Which activities from the video do you do? Which would you like to do?
3 When you are older, what kind of lifestyle will you have?

LISTENING

LISTENING 1

PREPARING TO LISTEN

USING YOUR
KNOWLEDGE

1 Work with a partner. Discuss your answers.

Each week, how much time do you spend
- with friends?
- on your cell phone?
- on your computer?

UNDERSTANDING
KEY VOCABULARY

2 Match photos a–g to the sentences.

1 I like to **play computer games**. They are fun and exciting. _____
2 I feel good and have more energy when I **exercise**. _____
3 I am very tired and need to rest. I'm going to **sleep** well tonight. _____
4 I **watch TV** on Thursday nights. My favorite show comes on at 7 p.m. _____
5 I like to **go online** and shop. I don't like going to stores—it takes too long. _____
6 I need to **do homework** tonight. I don't have time before school tomorrow. _____
7 I like to **text** friends because it is quicker than email. _____

PRONUNCIATION FOR LISTENING

Intonation in questions

Intonation is the way your voice goes up and down when you speak.

Your voice goes up ↗ when you ask *yes / no* questions. Your voice goes down ↘ when you ask *information* questions or make a statement.

A: What's your name? ↘   B: My name is Jennifer. ↘
A: Are you from New York? ↗   B: No. I'm from Toronto. ↘

3 ▶ 3.1 Listen to the dialogue from the skills box and repeat.

4 ▶ 3.2 Look at the questions and statements. Will the intonation go up or down? Write ↗ or ↘ in the boxes. Then listen and check.

1 What do you want to watch on TV? ☐
2 How many hours do you sleep every night? ☐
3 Who's between the ages of 13 and 19? ☐
4 Do you play computer games? ☐
5 It's important for people to exercise. ☐
6 Do you text a lot? ☐

PRISM Online Workbook

WHILE LISTENING

Listening for main ideas

If you listen for the main idea(s), you try to understand these questions:

- Where are the speakers? (e.g., a university, a hospital, a hotel)
- Who are the speakers? (e.g., family, friends, teacher and students)
- Why are they speaking? (e.g., They need information., They want help., They want to teach something.)

> **GLOSSARY**
>
> **lifestyle** (n) the way that you live
>
> **teenagers** (n) someone who is between 13 and 19 years old

LISTENING FOR MAIN IDEAS

PRISM Online Workbook

5 ▶ 3.3 Listen to a discussion. Put a check (✔) next to the correct answer.

1 The discussion is
   a in a supermarket. ☐
   b in a classroom. ☐
   c in a restaurant. ☐

2 The discussion is between a teacher and
   a students who exercise. ☐
   b students who do homework. ☐
   c all students in the class. ☐

3 The discussion is about
   a busy students. ☐
   b Saturday and Sunday. ☐
   c lifestyles. ☐

LISTENING FOR DETAILS

6 ▶ 3.3 Listen again. Write *T* (true) or *F* (false) next to the statements.

_____ 1 It's the afternoon.
_____ 2 The students are teenagers.
_____ 3 Jose sleeps 10 hours every night.
_____ 4 Maria usually watches TV at night.
_____ 5 Jiang watches TV or goes online on Saturday and Sunday.
_____ 6 Eunji exercises.

DISCUSSION

7 Work with a partner. Ask and answer the questions.

1 What healthy things do you do?
2 Do people usually exercise in your culture?
3 In your culture, do teachers usually ask questions about your life?

THE SIMPLE PRESENT

LANGUAGE

Statements

Use the simple present to talk about regular activities. Use the base form of the verb with *I / you / we / they*. Add *-s* or *-es* to the verb after *he / she / it*.

	singular		plural
I You We They	**go** at 8:30.	He She It	**goes** at 8:30.

For the negative, use *I / you / we / they* + *do* + *not* before the base form of the verb.
Use *he / she / it* + *does* + *not* before the base form of the verb.

	singular		plural
I You We They	do **not go** at 8:30. **don't go** at 8:30.	He She It	does **not go** at 8:30. **doesn't go** at 8:30.

Have is irregular:
I / You / We / They **have** a friend in London.
He / She / It **has** a friend in London.

PRISM Online Workbook

1 Circle the correct form of the verb in the simple present.

Peter and Barbara [1]*have / has* busy lifestyles. Peter [2]*get up / gets up* at 6:00 every morning and [3]*go / goes* to school. He usually [4]*don't eat / doesn't eat* breakfast but [5]*have coffee / has coffee* before his class [6]*start / starts*. Barbara [7]*don't go / doesn't go* to school. She [8]*work / works* in a store. Peter [9]*take / takes* the bus to school, but Barbara [10]*walk / walks* to work. Sometimes, at night, they both [11]*make dinner / makes dinner*. Then, Peter usually [12]*do / does* homework, and Barbara [13]*exercise / exercises*. In his free time, Peter [14]*play / plays* computer games, and Barbara [15]*go / goes* online. On the weekends, they [16]*don't like / doesn't like* to study or work.

Questions

Use *do* or *does* with the base form of the verb to ask *yes / no* questions.

yes / no questions				short answers	
do / does	subject	base form of verb		yes	no
Do	you	cook?		Yes, I **do**.	No, I **don't**.
Does	he	go	to the gym?	Yes, he **does**.	No, he **doesn't**.

Information questions begin with a *wh-* word. They ask for information and cannot be answered with *yes* or *no*.

information questions			
wh- word	*do / does*	subject	base form of verb
Who / What / When / How / Why	do	I / you /we / they	live? / work? / study?
Who / What / When / How / Why	does	he / she / it	live? / work? / study?

2 Put the words in the correct order to make questions.

1 exercise / you / Do?

_____

2 you / homework / do / Do / ?

_____

3 do / Which / computer games / play / you / ?

_____

4 in the evening / Do / watch / TV / you / ?

_____

5 Who / on the weekend / do / text / you / ?

_____

3 Correct the mistakes in the questions.

1 You cook food for your family?

_____

2 You do homework?

_____

3 What you do at home?

_____

4 Where go you with friends?

_____

5 What cell phone you like?

_____

VERB COLLOCATIONS

A *collocation* is a group of words that often go together. A collocation can be:
- a verb + noun / noun phrase: do homework, play computer games
- a verb + preposition phrase: go to the gym, eat at home
- a verb + adverb: go online

PRISM Online Workbook

4 Write the verbs from the box on the lines. Use the story about Peter and Barbara's lifestyle to help you.

get go ~~have~~ make play take watch

1 ___have___ a class / coffee
2 _____ breakfast / lunch / dinner
3 _____ soccer / computer games
4 _____ home / to school / to the gym
5 _____ up (in the morning)
6 _____ the bus
7 _____ TV / movies / videos

5 Write the verbs from the box in the table below.

| cook   do   eat   go   watch   have   play |

food	free time
• (1)_cook_____ food for your family	• **go out** with friends
• **eat out** at restaurants	• (4)_____ TV
• **have** coffee with friends	• **go** to the movies
• (2)_____ at home	• (5)_____ sports
• (3)_____ dinner with friends	• **play** computer games
• **make** lunch	• (6)_____ to the gym
	• **chat** online
	• (7)_____ homework

PREPARING TO LISTEN

USING YOUR KNOWLEDGE

1 Work with a partner. Discuss the questions about your country.

1 Do people talk to strangers on the street?
2 Do students usually live with their parents?
3 Do students have a lot of free time?

UNDERSTANDING KEY VOCABULARY

PRISM Online Workbook

2 Use the words in the box to complete the sentences.

---

busy (adj) if you are busy, you are doing a lot

café (n) a small restaurant for tea, coffee, and snacks

go out (v) to spend time with friends outside your home

gym (n) a place where you can go to exercise and get in shape

parent (n) your mother or father

study (v) to learn a particular subject, either in a school or college or by reading books

---

1 I have a test on Friday. I need to _____ on Thursday.
2 I like to exercise. I go to the _____ every day.
3 Alan and Kate both work, so they usually don't have time to make dinner. They _____ to a restaurant every night.
4 I have dinner with my _____ on Sundays. They miss me because I no longer live at home.
5 We go to a _____ and have coffee every week.
6 My life is very _____ . I almost don't have time to sleep.

3 When you ask and answer questions, it's important to use polite (friendly) words. Circle the polite words and phrases.

1 **A:** Excuse me. I'd like to ask you a question.
   B: Don't talk to me. Not now.
2 **A:** Can I have a few minutes of your time?
   B: Sure. No problem.
3 **A:** Pardon me. Do you have a minute?
   B: No. Sorry, I don't.

4 ▶ 3.4 Listen to the dialogues. Practice with a partner.

WHILE LISTENING

5 ▶ 3.5 Listen to an interview and answer the questions.

1 Where are the speakers?
   a in a university
   b in a café
   c on the street
2 Who are the speakers?
   a two strangers
   b a teacher and a student
   c good friends
3 What does April want to know about?
   a lifestyles
   b computer games
   c gyms

LISTENING FOR
MAIN IDEAS

6 ▶ 3.5 Listen again. Write Jasvinder's answers in the questionnaire.

QUESTIONNAIRE

Name: Jasvinder   **Job:** university student

A Home / Family

A1   Do you live with your parents?   Y ○   N ○

B Work / Studies

B1   Do you work or study?   work ○   study ○

B2   What's your job? / What do you study?   biology

C Lifestyle

C1   Do you have a busy lifestyle?   Y ○   N ○

C2a   How do you relax?

C2b   Do you like to exercise?   Y ○   N ○

C2c   Do you go to a gym?   Y ○   N ○

C2d   Do you go to the movies?   Y ○   N ○

C3a   When do you go out with friends?

C3b   Where do you go with your friends?

DISCUSSION

7 Work with a partner. Think of Listening 1 and Listening 2 and answer the questions.

1   In Listening 1, what things do the students do?
2   In Listening 2, what things does Jasvinder do?
3   Who has a busier lifestyle, the students or Jasvinder? Explain your answer.
4   Is your lifestyle like the students' or Jasvinder's? How?

SPEAKING

CRITICAL THINKING

At the end of this unit, you are going to do the Speaking Task below.

> Interview students for a survey.

> **Using surveys**
>
> In a survey, you use questions to find out information. For example, you can ask questions to learn about the lifestyles of students in your school or college.

1 Before you write your survey, think of the information April asks about in her survey in Listening 2. Write the topics from her questionnaire and the information from her questions in the idea map below.

ANALYZE ▲

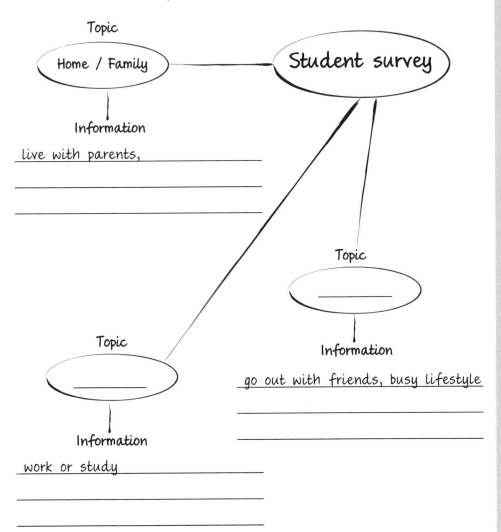

Topic

Home / Family — Student survey

Information

live with parents, _____

Topic

_____

Information

go out with friends, busy lifestyle

Topic

_____

Information

work or study

2 Make a survey for a student interview.

Think of topics and information you want to know about for your student survey. Write your topics in the circles of the idea map. Write the information you want to know about under your topics, e.g., go out with friends, play computer games, etc. Use ideas from Listening 1 and Listening 2 to help you.

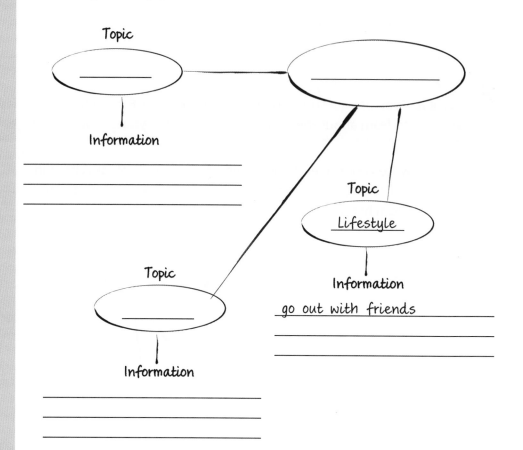

3 Write the information from your idea map in the question forms below to make questions for your questionnaire.

Yes / no questions: Do you ... ?

Information questions: Where do you _____ ?

                        When do you _____ ?

                        Why do you _____ ?

                        How do you _____ ?

                        Who do you _____ with?

4 Add more questions.

_____

_____

_____

PREPOSITIONS OF TIME

LANGUAGE

Use prepositions to talk about when something happens.

in + parts of the day	**in** the morning, **in** the afternoon, **in** the evening
	I play computer games **in** the evening.
at + clock time	**at** 7:30, **at** 12:00, **at** 1:00 p.m.
	Luis eats dinner **at** 7:30.
on + day of the week	**on** Monday, **on** Tuesday, **on** Wednesday
	She exercises **on** Monday and Wednesday.

1 Read the sentences below. Underline

- *in* + parts of the day.
- *at* + clock time.
- *on* + day of the week.

1 Fahd has breakfast <u>at 6:30</u> <u>in the morning</u>.
2 Tania gets up at 6:00 in the morning.
3 Chen and Wang watch movies on Tuesdays in the evening.
4 My sister makes my lunch on Wednesdays.
5 Luis goes home at 3:00 in the afternoon.
6 I play soccer with my friends on Saturdays.

2 Read this text about a student. Write *in*, *on*, or *at* in the blanks.

    This is Claudia. She's from Canada. She takes the bus to
the university every day. The bus comes (1)_____ 7:30.
Claudia arrives (2)_____ 8:30. She has a biology class
(3)_____ nine (4)_____ Tuesday and Thursday.
(5)_____ Wednesday, she has lunch with her friends
(6)_____ 12:30. (7)_____ Thursday, Claudia has an
English class (8)_____ three o'clock (9)_____ the
afternoon. She goes to the movies with her family
(10)_____ Friday evening. (11)_____ Saturday, she
exercises (12)_____ the morning. (13)_____ Sunday,
she does her homework (14)_____ the evening.
She has a busy week.

3 ▶ 3.6 Listen and check your answers.

PRONUNCIATION FOR SPEAKING

Simple present -s and -es endings

You say /s/ after the sounds /t/, /p/, /k/, and /f/—texts, sleeps, takes, gets, laughs.

You say /z/ after /d/, /l/, /b/, /g/, /v/, /m/, /n/, /r/, and all vowel sounds—needs, calls, wears, goes, has, studies, plays.

You say /əz/ after /z/, /tʃ/, /ʃ/, /s/, and /dʒ/—chooses, watches, teaches, misses.

PRISM Online Workbook

4 ▶ 3.7 Listen and repeat.

5 ▶ 3.7 Listen again. Write the number of syllables next to each word.

texts _____   sleeps _____   needs _____   goes _____
studies _____   watches _____   chooses _____

6 ▶ 3.8 Listen and check (✔) the box with the ending you hear.

	/s/	/z/	/əz/
1 gets	✔		
2 wears			
3 misses			
4 has			
5 teaches			
6 takes			
7 plays			
8 laughs			

Interview students for a survey.

PREPARE

1 Look back at your questions in Critical Thinking. Review your questions and add any new information you want to include.

2 Use the polite ways in the boxes to ask and answer questions in your interview.

Asking	Answering
• Excuse me! Can I ask you some questions?	• Yes, sure. / Yes, no problem.
• I'm ... What's your name?	• Yes. / Yes, I think so.
• I'm ...	• No. / No, not really.
• Nice to meet you!	
• OK, do you ... ?	

3 Refer to the Task Checklist as you prepare your interview.

TASK CHECKLIST	✔
Create questions for a survey.	
Use the simple present to ask and answer questions.	
Use the correct simple present -s and -es endings.	

DISCUSS

4 Work in groups. Interview a student from your group. Take notes to remember your partner's answers to the questions.

5 Work with a partner from another group. Tell your new partner about your first partner's answers. Remember to add -s or -es to your simple present verbs.

ON CAMPUS

TIME MANAGEMENT

PREPARING TO LISTEN

1 You are going to listen to some college students describing their schedules. Before you listen, discuss the questions with a partner.

1 How do you think college students spend their time?
2 Why is it difficult for some students to find time to study?
3 How can students find more time to study?

SKILLS

Time management

As a student, you will have many things to do, so it is important to organize your time well. Time management is making sure you find time in your busy life for the important things like studying.

WHILE LISTENING

2 ▶ 3.9 Listen to Joe, Fabiola, and Michaela. Which student has the least free time? Which student has the most?

3 ▶ 3.9 Listen again. Check (✔) the correct box to complete each sentence.

		Joe	Fabiola	Michaela
1	stays up late.			
2	gets up early every day.			
3	has a job.			
4	studies in the mornings.			
5	studies in the dorm.			
6	studies in the library.			
7	can't study on weekends.			

4 Work with a partner. Talk about the questions.

1 How is Joe's lifestyle different from Fabiola's and Michaela's?
2 In your opinion, which student has the best lifestyle? Why?
3 Which student is most similar to you?

PRACTICE

Strategies for time management ⏰

- [ ] Get up and go to bed at the same times every day.
- [ ] Make a list of what you have to do.
- [ ] Use a calendar or a planner to organize your time.
- [ ] Schedule extra time to study for tests or work on group projects.
- [ ] Turn off social media and email.

5 Read the strategies for time management and check (✔) the ones you use.

6 Read the students' problems. Decide which strategy (or strategies) would help with each problem?

1. I never have enough time to study. I always have so much to do!

2. I start to do some work—and then I spend an hour chatting to my friends online!

3. Oh, no! I have a paper due tomorrow ... and two quizzes!

4. I stayed up late to do my homework last night, and now I'm really tired.

5. I completely forgot the homework assignment. Now I'm going to get a bad grade!

REAL-WORLD APPLICATION

7 Work with a partner. Ask and answer the questions.

1. Do you get up and go to bed at the same times every day?
2. Do you make a list of things to do?
3. Do you use a planner or a calendar?
4. When is the best time for you to study?
5. Do you turn off social media when you are studying?

8 Choose **one** of the questions in Exercise 7. Ask as many students as possible the question. Make notes of the answers.

9 Tell the class about the answers.

Six people use a planner. Two people use an online calendar...

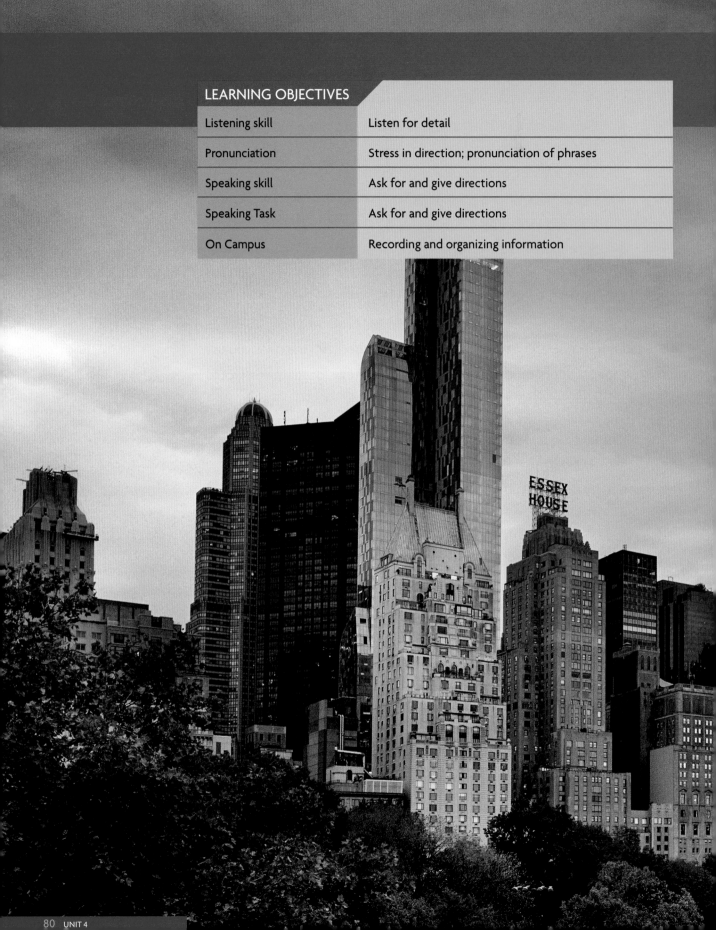

LEARNING OBJECTIVES

Listening skill	Listen for detail
Pronunciation	Stress in direction; pronunciation of phrases
Speaking skill	Ask for and give directions
Speaking Task	Ask for and give directions
On Campus	Recording and organizing information

ESSEX HOUSE

ACTIVATE YOUR KNOWLEDGE

Work with a partner. Ask and answer the questions.

1 What can you see in the photo?
2 Have you been to a place like this?
3 Is it similar to somewhere in your country?

WATCH AND LISTEN

PREPARING TO WATCH

ACTIVATING YOUR
KNOWLEDGE

1 Work with a partner. Discuss the questions.

1 Do you live in a big city or a small town?
2 How is a city different from a small town?
3 Why do people move to cities?
4 How do cities change?

PREDICTING CONTENT
USING VISUALS

2 Look at the pictures from the video. Match the sentences to the photos (1–4).

a The man is taking a picture. _____
b Many Asian cities have large populations. _____
c The city is changing. It is growing. _____
d In the past, the city was smaller. _____

GLOSSARY

grow (v) to become larger, to increase in size or amount

record (n) information or a description of an event, usually on paper or in pictures

skyline (n) the outline of buildings, mountains, etc., against the sky

tower (n) a tall, thin building or structure, for example, the Eiffel Tower in Paris, France, and the CN Tower in Toronto, Canada

urban (adj) of or in a city

WHILE WATCHING

3 ▶ Watch the video. Write *T* (true) or *F* (false) next to the statements below.

UNDERSTANDING
MAIN IDEAS

_____ 1 More people live in cities today.

_____ 2 Shanghai is one of China's biggest cities.

_____ 3 Mr. Yao takes pictures of Shanghai once a year.

_____ 4 The city does not look very different today.

4 ▶ Watch again. Write the missing information.

UNDERSTANDING
DETAILS

1 In 1970, only two cities in the world had more than _____ million people.

2 These urban areas are _____ for our future.

3 He takes pictures of the Shanghai skyline to make a record of _____ in his hometown.

4 Today the city looks very _____ .

5 Circle the correct answer. Then compare your answers with a partner.

MAKING INFERENCES

1 There are more jobs in *cities / small towns*.

2 China has *slow-growing / fast-growing* cities.

3 People *do not like / like* to record changes.

4 Cities often change *a little / a lot*.

DISCUSSION

6 Work with a partner. Discuss the questions.

1 Has your hometown changed? How has it changed?

2 What is the tallest building in your city?

3 Why do you think cities change?

LISTENING

LISTENING 1

PREPARING TO LISTEN

1 You are going to listen to a presentation about a new cell phone app. Use the words in the box to complete the sentences.

> **building** (n) a house, school, hospital, or office
> **directions** (n) information that tells you how to get to a place
> **library** (n) a place where people can come to study and that has a lot of books for people to take home
> **location** (n) where something is
> **map** (n) a picture that shows where countries, towns, roads, rivers, etc. are
> **safe** (adj) not dangerous

1 What is the exact _____ of New York City? Is it in the east or west of the country?
2 I need a quiet place to study and read. I'm going to the _____ after school.
3 This is a dangerous area. It's not _____ to walk here alone at night.
4 I have the _____ to find your house. They look easy. I will be there in 20 minutes.
5 This is a big city. There are a lot of tall _____ .
6 Do you see my country on the _____ ? It's right there. It's very small.

PRONUNCIATION FOR LISTENING

Stress in directions

Stress the words

- *this* and *here* to point to things that are near.
- *that* and *there* to point to things that are not near.

2 ▶ 4.1 Listen. Write the words you hear to complete the sentences.

   1 Where is _____ photo from?

   2 … there's a store _____ and a library _____ .

   3 Yes, that's a bank over _____ .

   4 The library is _____ .

3 ▶ 4.1 Listen again. Are the words you wrote stressed?

4 Work with a partner. Look at the map and discuss the questions.

   1 What do you use this map for?

   2 Where can you find this map?

   3 What places can you see on the map?

USING YOUR
KNOWLEDGE

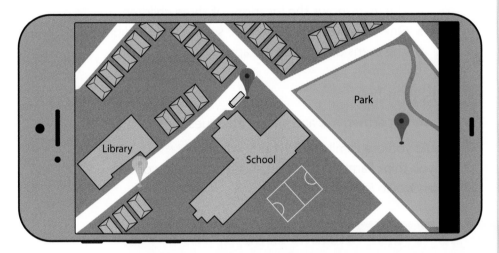

WHILE LISTENING

5 ▶ 4.2 Listen to the presentation. Choose the correct answers.

   1 Familynet is

     a an app for children.

     b an app for work.

     c an app that can find everyone in the family.

   2 The presenter says that the map is of

     a his home.

     b his daughters' school.

     c the locations of his children.

   3 The presentation is about

     a how to be safe.

     b how to make parents and children happy.

     c how to find everyone in your family.

LISTENING FOR
MAIN IDEAS

Listening for details

A *detail* is a fact about something. A detail can be

- a number, a letter, an address.
- a question or instruction.
- an example of something.

6 ▶ 4.2 Listen again. Write *T* (true) or *F* (false) next to the statements.

_____ 1 Parents and children are very busy.
_____ 2 The app works all the time.
_____ 3 The app shows locations.
_____ 4 The map shows the locations of three children.
_____ 5 One daughter is between the school and the library.
_____ 6 The teens do not like the app.

DISCUSSION

7 Work with a partner. Ask and answer the questions.

1 Would you use Familynet? Why or why not?
2 Do you think Familynet keeps children safe? Why or why not?
3 When would Familynet not work?

⊙ LANGUAGE DEVELOPMENT

VOCABULARY FOR PLACES

1 Match the words to the places on the map.

> **bank** (n) somewhere you can put your money
> **bridge** (n) something that goes over water so people can get from one side to the other
> **factory** (n) a place where workers use machines to make things
> **fountain** (n) a beautiful tower with water coming out of it
> **library** (n) a place with a lot of books
> **monument** (n) something large that people visit to remember an important person or event
> **museum** (n) a place with paintings, statues, and important things from history
> **park** (n) a place you can go for a walk and see a lot of trees and grass
> **train station** (n) somewhere you can get on a train
> **university** (n) a place where students study at a high level after high school

Map 1

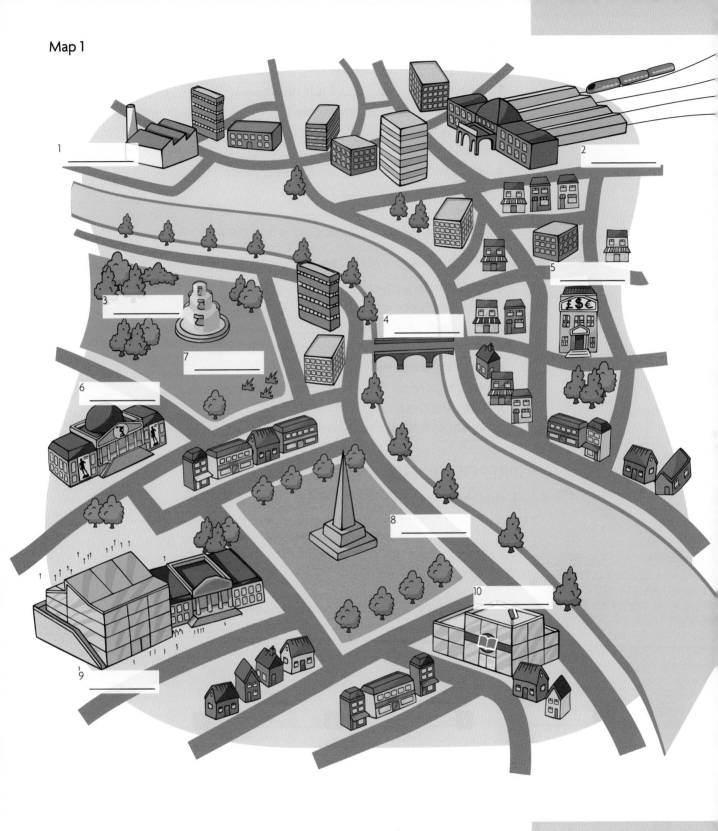

1 _____

2 _____

3 _____

4 _____

5 _____

6 _____

7 _____

8 _____

9 _____

10 _____

2 ▶ 4.3 Listen to eight short conversations. Write the words you hear to complete the sentences.

1 Where's the _____ ? Is it near here?
2 Is there a _____ near here?
3 Where's the famous _____ ?
4 Excuse me. Where's the _____ ?
5 I can't find the _____ . Is it near here?
6 Where's the _____ ?
7 Where can I find the _____ ?
8 I'm looking for the _____ . Is it in the park?

3 ▶ 4.3 Listen again. Match each question from Exercise 2 to an answer.

a Yes, it's behind the river. _____
b Yes. There's one over the bridge. Can you see it? _____
c It's in front of a tall building. _____
d It's between the university and the river. _____
e Yes. It's there in the park. _____
f No. It's there on the left. It's next to the park. _____
g It's by the river. _____
h It's across from those houses. _____

PREPOSITIONS OF PLACE

4 Find these prepositions in Exercise 3 and circle them.

| by | behind | between | in | in front of |
| next to | on the left / right | across from | over |

5 Write the prepositions from the box under the pictures.

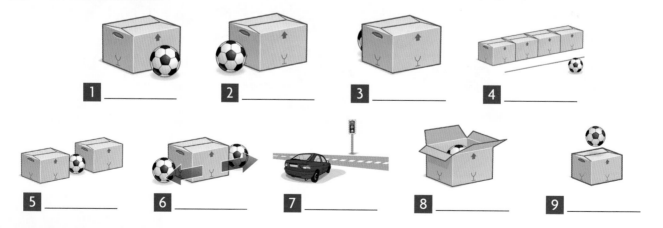

1 _____
2 _____
3 _____
4 _____
5 _____
6 _____
7 _____
8 _____
9 _____

6 Look at Map 2. Write words from the pictures below and Exercise 5 to complete the sentences.

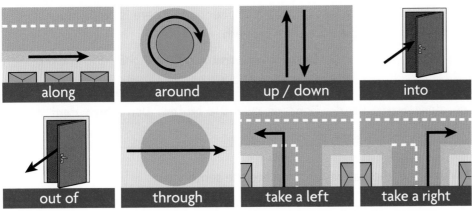

| along | around | up / down | into |
| out of | through | take a left | take a right |

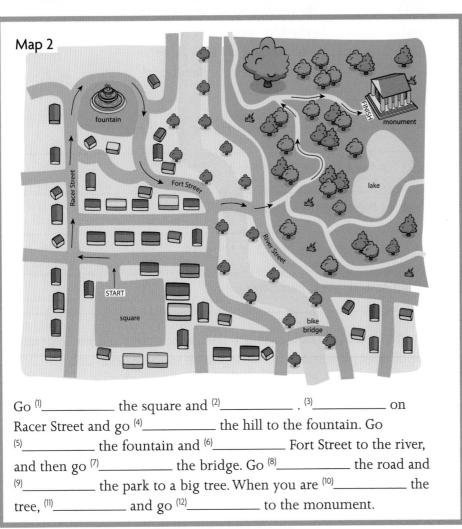

Map 2

Go (1)_____ the square and (2)_____ . (3)_____ on Racer Street and go (4)_____ the hill to the fountain. Go (5)_____ the fountain and (6)_____ Fort Street to the river, and then go (7)_____ the bridge. Go (8)_____ the road and (9)_____ the park to a big tree. When you are (10)_____ the tree, (11)_____ and go (12)_____ to the monument.

THE IMPERATIVE

Use the imperative to give instructions and directions. There is no pronoun in the imperative. Use the base form of the verb.

Go along South Road.   **Go** over the bridge. **Turn** right at the bank.

Use *do not / don't* with the imperative to make the negative

Don't go along South Road. **Don't go** over the bridge. **Don't turn** right at the bank.

PRISM Online Workbook

7 Write the imperative to complete the sentences.

1 (Go) _____ left on Small Street.
2 (Walk) _____ down Main Road to get to the bus station.
3 (Take) _____ a right on Sun Street to get to the park.
4 (Enter) _____ the building on York Street.
5 (Don't forget) _____ to get the directions!

8 Correct the sentences.

1 You turn the map the other way, please! I can't read it.

_____

2 Looks for the café on South Road.

_____

3 No enter the building on Main Road.

_____

4 Don't to go along York Street to the gym.

_____

5 Not go east on West Park Street.

_____

9 Work with a partner. Look at Map 2. Use prepositions and the imperative to give different directions from the square to the monument.

PREPARING TO LISTEN

1 Work with a partner. Ask and answer the questions.

   a In what places do people get lost (not know where they are)?
   b What can they do to find their way again?

USING YOUR
KNOWLEDGE

2 Work with a partner. Ask the questions about places in the chart. Add more places if you can.

- Which of these places did you go to last week?
- Were the places difficult to find?

UNDERSTANDING
KEY VOCABULARY

PRISM Online Workbook

food court—a place with many small restaurants, usually in a shopping mall	**shopping mall**—a building with many different kinds of stores inside
parking lot—an area for cars	**playground**—a place with special equipment for children to play on
movie theater—a place where people go to watch movies	**hospital**—a place to get help if you are sick or hurt
campus—a large area for university buildings	**restrooms**—rooms in a public building where there are toilets
supermarket—a large store with food to buy	**department store**—a store with a lot of different things, such as clothes, towels, furniture, toys, etc.
_____	
_____	
_____	

3 You are going to listen to some students answer questions about directions. Before you listen, look at Map 3. What kind of place can you see? Circle the correct answer.

a a map of a shopping mall
b a map of a university campus
c a map of a small town

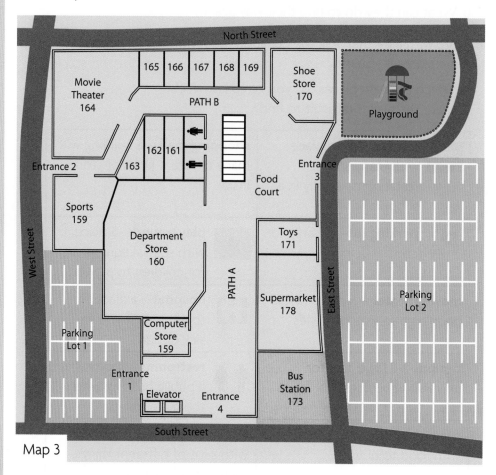

Map 3

4 Look at the map. Write *T* (true) or *F* (false) next to the statements.

_____ **1** There are two parking lots.
_____ **2** There are stairs and an elevator in the shopping mall.
_____ **3** The supermarket is between the bus station and South Street.
_____ **4** The playground is behind the shoe store.
_____ **5** Entrance 3 is on North Street.
_____ **6** The food court is across from the stairs.
_____ **7** The restrooms are in front of the stairs.
_____ **8** There is a bus station on East Street.

WHILE LISTENING

5 ▶ 4.4 Listen to some students give directions. Choose the correct answers.

1 The students are
   a at a shopping mall.
   b lost.
   c looking at a map.
2 The teacher thinks it's important to
   a know how to find shopping malls.
   b understand map directions.
   c like shopping.
3 Who asks the questions?
   a the teacher
   b the students
   c the teacher and the students

6 ▶ 4.4 Listen again. Write the words you hear to complete the sentences.

1 Pedro, I'm at the department store. How do I get to the _____ ?
2 Pedro: Go _____ the store and take a _____ on path A.
3 Hongmi, I'm on North Street. Can you tell me how to get to the _____ ?
4 Hongmi: Yes, go _____ . Then, take a _____ on East Street and follow it until you see the supermarket. It's on your right, _____ to the bus station.
5 Excuse me, miss. Where is the _____ ?
6 Luisa: Oh, that's easy. It's _____ from you _____ to the stairs.

DISCUSSION

7 Work with a partner. Discuss the questions.

1 In Listening 1, a family uses an app to find each other. In Listening 2, students use a map to find locations in a shopping mall. Would you use the Familynet app in the shopping mall? Why or why not?
2 What do you do when you get lost on the street? In a shopping mall? In a parking lot?
3 In Listening 1 and Listening 2, the speakers use words that are used to give directions in the U.S. In your culture, when you give directions, do you use
   • street names and numbers?
   • miles for distance?
   • north, south, east, and west?
4 Do you like to use an app or a map when you travel to a new place? Why or why not?

CRITICAL THINKING

At the end of this unit, you are going to do the Speaking Task below.

> Ask for and give directions in a college town.

UNDERSTAND

1 Circle the words used to describe locations in the sentences.

along	at	behind	in	here	next to	on

across from   right / left   through   then   there   this

  1 The movie theater is (on your right.)
  2 I'm in this shoe store.
  3 It's there, on your right, next to the bus station.
  4 It's here behind the food court and the shoe store.
  5 I'm at the movie theater.
  6 It's across from you next to the stairs.

2 Work with a partner. Look at map 3 of the shopping mall on page 92. Use arrows to draw the way from parking lot 1 to the playground.

APPLY

3 Use the directions to describe the way from parking lot 1 to the playground in the correct order.

- When you get to the food court, take a right / take a left.
- Go in entrance 1 / entrance 2 / entrance 3.
- At path A / path B, ...
- Take a left / right.
- It's here / there.
- It's in front of the shoe store / behind the shoe store.
- Go along path A / path B.

_____

_____

_____

_____

_____

4 Work with a partner. Answer the questions.

  a How do I get from Entrance 2 to the elevator?
  b How do I get from the bus station to the shoe store?

SPEAKING

PREPARATION FOR SPEAKING

GIVING DIRECTIONS

> SKILLS
>
> Give directions by using imperatives, prepositions, and describing locations.

1 Look at the directions from Listening 2. Underline the imperatives used to give directions.

1 <u>Go</u> out of the store and <u>take</u> a left on path A.
2 Go east. Then, take a right on East Street and follow it until you see the supermarket.
3 Go along path B and go through the food court.

2 ▶ 4.5 Listen and write the words from the box to complete the sentences.

> along   at   behind   in   in front of
> next to   on   across from   right   through

1 It's _____ the business school.
2 It's _____ Green Square.
3 Go _____ Alpha Park to the Student Center.
4 It's _____ front of that big fountain. There—on the _____ .
5 OK, then, so we're _____ the language school.
6 Go _____ French Road.
7 There's one _____ the train station.
8 It's there _____ the left. It's _____ that school.

ASKING FOR DIRECTIONS

3 ▶ 4.6 Put the words in the correct order. Then listen and check your answers.

1 the / Where's / supermarket / ?
2 Is the / here / physics building / near / ?
3 the language center / How/ do I / get to / ?
4 how to get / to the history / Can you tell me / building / ?
5 the math building / I'm looking for / . / near here / Is it / ?

PRISM Online Workbook

PRISM Online Workbook

4 ▶ 4.7 Listen to the words in the box and repeat.

> math building   physics building
> language center   student center

5 Work with a partner. Write the names of the places in the box to complete the sentences. Take turns asking for directions.

1 Excuse me. Where's the _____ ?
2 Can you tell me how to get to _____ ?
3 Is there a _____ near here?
4 How do I get to the _____ ?

6 ▶ 4.8 Listen to three people ask for directions. Write the questions that they ask.

a Excuse me! _____ , please?
b Excuse me! I think I'm lost. _____ ?
c Excuse me! _____ ?

PRONUNCIATION FOR SPEAKING

SKILLS

Pronunciation of phrases

A statement or question has one or more phrases. A phrase has one or two stressed words.

7 ▶ 4.9 Listen to these questions. Underline the words or parts of words with stress. (You will hear each phrase by itself, then the whole question.)

1 Excuse me!   Where's the   student center?
2 Excuse me!   I think I'm lost.   How do I get to   the chemistry building?
3 Excuse me!   Can you tell me   how to get to   the supermarket?

8 ▶ 4.9 Listen again. Does the voice go up or down in the phrases and questions? Write (↗ or ↘) in the spaces.

1 Excuse me! I think I'm lost. _____
2 Where's the student center, please? _____
3 How do I get to the chemistry building? _____
4 Can you tell me the way to the supermarket? _____

9 ▶ 4.9 Listen again. Repeat each phrase you hear. Then repeat the whole question.

SPEAKING TASK

▶ Ask for and give directions in a college town.

PREPARE

1 You are going to help a group of new students at your college. Look back at Preparation for Speaking for language you want to include.

2 Refer to the Task Checklist as you prepare your directions.

TASK CHECKLIST	✔
Ask for directions.	
Give directions and use the correct order.	
Use the imperative.	
Use words and phrases to describe location (e.g., *behind*, *on*, *in*, etc.).	
Practice your pronunciation of phrases and stress the correct word.	

PRACTICE

3 Work in two groups, A and B.

Group A: Go to page 193.
Group B: Go to page 195.

DISCUSS

4 Work with a student from the other group.

Student A: Look at the map of The University of Beta. Ask Student B for directions to the places below (1–5). Write the correct letter (A–E) next to each place.

Student B: Look at the map on page 194. Give directions to Student A.

The University of Beta

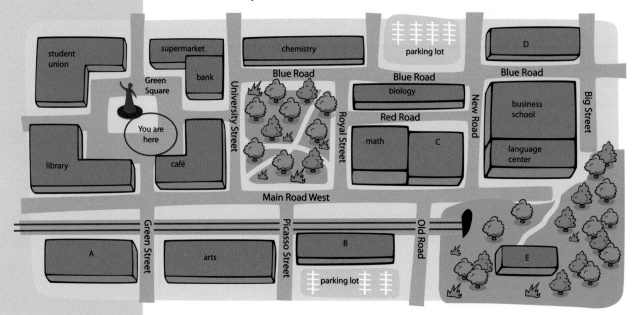

1 the history building _____
2 the train station _____
3 the physics building _____
4 the bus station _____
5 the gym _____

5 Change roles.

Student B: Look at the map of The University of Alpha. Ask Student A for directions to the places below (1–5). Write the correct letter (A–E) next to each place.

Student A: Look at the map on page 192. Give directions to Student B.

The University of Alpha

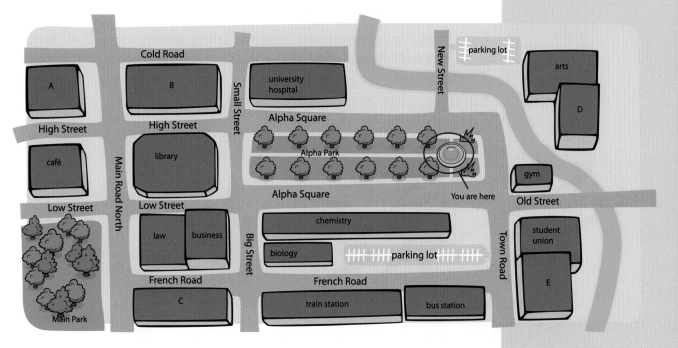

1 the bank _____
2 the language center _____
3 the physics building _____
4 the history building _____
5 the supermarket _____

6 Use the maps on pages 192 and 194 to check your answers together.

ON CAMPUS

RECORDING AND ORGANIZING INFORMATION

PREPARING TO LISTEN

1 You are going to listen to some teachers talking about things that students often need for school. Look at the pictures of school supplies and answer the questions.

    1 Which things do you use regularly?
    2 What do you use them for?
    3 Which do you never use? Why not?

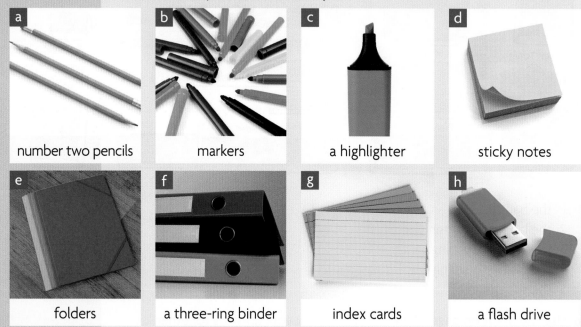

| a number two pencils | b markers | c a highlighter | d sticky notes |
| e folders | f a three-ring binder | g index cards | h a flash drive |

WHILE LISTENING

2 ▶ 4.10 Listen to the professors' instructions. Write the things that the students will need.

    1 _____   3 _____   5 _____
    2 _____   4 _____

3 ▶ 4.10 Match each item from Exercise 2 with its purpose. Then listen again and check your answers.

    1 a number two pencil   a to move files from one computer to another
    2 a highlighter   b to organize papers and handouts
    3 a three-ring binder   c to write notes on for a presentation
    4 a flash drive   d to take tests
    5 index cards   e to mark important information

Recording and organizing information

Students have to learn a lot of information. Use highlighters, folders and other materials to help you record, remember, and organize your notes.

PRACTICE

4 Read the questions. Check (✔) the replies that are true for you. You can check more than one reply for each question.

1 When you are in a class, how do you take notes?

I listen carefully and try to write down every word.

I only write down the most important things.

I ask my classmate for the notes after class.

I don't write anything—I can usually remember it.

2 How do you organize papers and handouts?

I use three-ring binders and folders to organize things.

I just keep everything in one place.

I can never find anything!

I throw away the papers after class.

3 How do you prefer to read material for class?

I prefer to read things on paper or from a textbook.

I prefer to read on a computer screen.

I read carefully and highlight important points.

I don't like to read at all!

4 How do you remember vocabulary and important words?

I write new words in a notebook.

I write words on index cards.

I use a computer application to learn new words.

I try to use new words as much as possible.

5 Work in small groups. Compare your answers. Who has good study habits?

REAL-WORLD APPLICATION

6 Work with a partner. What stationery would you use for each of the study tasks below?

1 You have a history quiz next week, and you want to make sure you remember important names and dates.

2 You are working on a group project. You have some large electronic files that you want to share with the other members of your group.

3 You are studying a chapter in the textbook, and you want to clearly show the information you will need for a quiz next week.

4 For a writing assignment, you have to print and give your professor several drafts of your paper.

Work in small groups. Are your ideas the same?

LEARNING OBJECTIVES

Listening skill	Use your knowledge to predict content
Pronunciation	Weak form of *have to* and *should*; weak sounds in comparatives
Speaking skill	Ask for and give opinions and reasons
Speaking Task	Choose a person for a job
On Campus	Asking politely

ACTIVATE YOUR KNOWLEDGE

1 Which job can you see in the photo?

2 Which adjectives describe the job in the photo?

boring dangerous difficult easy interesting safe

3 Would you like to do this job? Why or why not?

ACTIVATING YOUR
KNOWLEDGE

PREPARING TO WATCH

1 Match the building and the city.

1	Empire State Building	a	Dubai
2	Eiffel Tower	b	New York
3	Burj Khalifa	c	Kuala Lumpur
4	Petronas Towers	d	Paris

PREDICTING CONTENT
USING VISUALS

2 Look at the pictures from the video. Put the words in order to make sentences.

1 very / is / tall / The building / .
2 beautiful view / This building / a / has / .
3 The man / a / very dangerous / job / has / .
4 work / together / These / men / .

> **GLOSSARY**
>
> **careful** (adj) giving attention to something
>
> **dirty** (adj) not clean
>
> **exciting** (adj) making you feel interested; not boring
>
> **ground** (n) the surface of the Earth

WHILE WATCHING

3 ▶ Watch the video. Circle the correct answer.

1 Where is the world's tallest building?
   a Beijing
   b Dubai
   c Mexico City

2 What is a problem with the building?
   a It is taller than any other building.
   b The men cannot clean it.
   c Its windows get dirty.

3 How long does it take to clean all the windows?
   a three months
   b fifteen days
   c one week

UNDERSTANDING
MAIN IDEAS

4 ▶ Watch again. Write *T* (true) or *F* (false) next to the statements.

_____ 1 The Burj Khalifa is over 1,800 meters tall.
_____ 2 The men work thousands of feet above the ground.
_____ 3 The men clean 24,000 doors.
_____ 4 Johnny's team has a dangerous, but exciting job.

UNDERSTANDING
DETAILS

5 Write the phrases from the box in the correct column of the table.

MAKING INFERENCES

have / has many offices   have / has a dangerous job
is / are very famous   need / needs special training

the window washers	the building
1 _____	3 _____
2 _____	4 _____

DISCUSSION

6 Work with a partner. Discuss the questions.

1 Do you, or someone you know, have a dangerous or exciting job? What is it?
2 What are some other dangerous jobs?
3 Why do you think some people like dangerous jobs?

LISTENING

LISTENING 1

PREPARING TO LISTEN

UNDERSTANDING KEY VOCABULARY

1 You are going to listen to a student who needs to decide what job to do. Write the words from the box to complete the sentences.

> **advice** (n) suggestions about what you think someone should do
> **boring** (adj) not interesting or exciting
> **earn** (v) to get money for doing work
> **hard** (adj) difficult to do or something that takes a lot of effort
> **help** (v) to make it easier for someone to do something
> **job** (n) the work a person does to get money
> **work** (v) to do a job, especially a job you do to get money

1 I have to _____ more hours this week because I was on vacation last week.

2 Who _____ more money—a doctor or an engineer?

3 She has a very good _____ . It pays well. She makes more money than I do.

4 She's a doctor. She _____ a lot of people get better when they are sick.

5 I don't think that job is interesting. It would be _____ to do it every day.

6 You have to study for many years and be good at science to become a doctor. That sounds _____ to me.

7 He has to decide what to do. He should ask his parents for _____ .

Using your knowledge to predict content

Before you listen to a talk or a conversation, answer these questions.

- What is the topic?
- What do you know about the topic?

Use your knowledge of the topic to help you understand.

USING YOUR
KNOWLEDGE

2 Work with a partner. Discuss your answers to the questions.

1 What is more important to you in a job? Use the words in the box to help you.

> helping others   kind of job   money   work hours

2 How do people choose their jobs?
3 Who do you talk to when you need to decide something important?

3 Match the jobs to the correct pictures.

1 business woman _____   4 doctor _____
2 chef _____   5 musician _____
3 engineer _____   6 scientist _____

4 Answer the questions about the jobs in Exercise 3. Use your own ideas.

Who
1 works harder than other people? *a chef*
2 helps people?
3 has a more interesting job?
4 earns more money?

PRONUNCIATION FOR LISTENING

Weak form *have to / should*

▶ 5.1 Words in a sentence are pronounced either with stress or no stress. The main verb, the subject, and object are usually stressed. Words like auxiliary verbs, prepositions, and articles are usually unstressed or weak forms.

The weak form /ə/ is very common in spoken and informal English. Look at the weak forms for *has to*, *have to*, and *should* in the box.

	strong form	weak form
has to	/hæz tʊ/	/həz tə/
have to	/ˈhæv tʊ/	/həv tə/
should	/ʃʊd/	/ʃəd/

5 ▶ 5.2 Listen and decide if *have to / has to / should* are in the weak or strong form.

1 I *have to* choose a course. *weak / strong*
2 *Should* I be a musician? *weak / strong*
3 He *has to* get some advice. *weak / strong*
4 You *have to* work hard. *weak / strong*
5 I *should* go to medical school. *weak / strong*
6 She *has to* decide what to do. *weak / strong*

WHILE LISTENING

> **GLOSSARY**
>
> **grade** (n) a number or letter that shows how good someone's work is
>
> **high school advisor** (n) someone who gives advice about jobs to high school students
>
> **medical school** (n) school where students study to become doctors

6 ▶ 5.3 Listen and circle the correct answers.

LISTENING FOR MAIN IDEAS

1 Who is the student with?
   a her friend
   b her high school advisor
   c her mother

2 What does the student ask for?
   a money
   b to be a musician
   c advice about what to study

7 ▶ 5.3 Listen again. Circle the correct answers.

LISTENING FOR DETAILS

1 Beatrice is going to college *next year / this year*.
2 There *are / aren't* many jobs for musicians.
3 Beatrice says a doctor's job is *good / boring*.
4 Beatrice's mother wants her to go to *engineering school / medical school*.
5 The advisor says Beatrice has *good grades / a good job*.
6 The advisor thinks Beatrice should *go to medical school / get a job*.

DISCUSSION

8 Work with a partner. Ask and answer the questions.

1 Would you like to do any of the jobs in Exercise 1? Why or why not?
2 What is your dream job?
3 What do you have to do to get this job?
4 In the U.S., students often start college, but don't know what they want to be. Sometimes they start to study to be a doctor, for example, but then decide to change. In your culture, do college students do this often? Why or why not?

⊙ LANGUAGE DEVELOPMENT

HAVE TO / HAS TO

Use *have to / has to* + base form of the verb to show that something is necessary.

I / you / we / they	have to	be	helpful.
He / she / it	has to	get up	early.

Nurses **have to be** helpful.
A teacher **has to get up** early.
Do doctors **have to be** polite?

Use *don't / doesn't have to* + base form of verb to show that something is not necessary.

I / you / we / they	do not / don't	have to	be	helpful.
He / she / it	does not / doesn't	have to	get up	early.

Nurses **don't have to be** women.
A doctor **doesn't have to work** in a hospital.

Use *do / does* + subject + *have to* + base form of the verb to ask if something is necessary.
Do we **have to** leave now?
Does she **have** to be a doctor?

1 ▶ 5.4 Complete the sentences with the words in the box. Listen and check.

| has   has to   have   have to |

1 Fatima _____ two jobs.
2 Mark _____ work very hard.
3 I _____ a very good job.
4 Engineers _____ a difficult job.
5 Paul _____ an important job.
6 Builders _____ work fast.

2 Correct the sentences below.

1 Students have read a lot of books.

_____

2 My teacher have to walk to school.

_____

3 You don't have study English.

_____

4 Teachers don't to work at night.

_____

5 Have we learn this grammar?

_____

6 What does a nurse has to do?

_____

3 Work with a partner. Choose one of these jobs. What do people in this job have to do?

| chef   journalist   scientist   soccer player |

4 Work with a new partner. Repeat Exercise 3, choosing a different job.

SHOULD

Use *should* + the base form of the verb to make suggestions or give advice.

I / you / he / she / we / they **should** go to medical school.

Use *should not/shouldn't* + the base form of the verb in the negative

I / you / he / she / we / they **should not** / **shouldn't** go to medical school.

5 Correct the sentences.

1 Paul should goes to engineering school.

_____

2 The advisor thinks that Beatrice not should get a job next year.

_____

3 Laura shoulds ask for advice from her friend.

_____

4 The students no shouldn't miss their classes.

_____

COMPARATIVE ADJECTIVES

Use comparative adjectives to compare two or more things.

Add *-er (than)* to one-syllable adjectives. Use *-ier (than)* with two-syllable adjectives with *-y*.	This job is saf**er** than that job. (safe → safer) This class is eas**ier** than my other class. (easy → easier)
Some adjectives double the consonant: *big → bigger*.	I am big**ger** than my yoga teacher. (big → bigger)
Adjectives with two or more syllables: Do not add *-er*. Say *more* + ADJECTIVE *(than)*.	Computer science is a **more interesting** job than medicine. (interesting → more interesting)
Irregular comparative adjectives: good → better (than), bad → worse (than).	If I have to choose, I think this job is **better** than that job. (good → better) This job is **worse** than the one I had before. (bad → worse)

6 ▶ **5.5** Listen and repeat the adjectives. Write the number of syllables you hear. Listen again and check your answers.

1 boring _____
2 interesting _____
3 safe _____
4 easy _____
5 difficult _____

6 nice _____
7 big _____
8 small _____
9 fast _____
10 important _____

7 Write the comparative form of the adjectives from Exercise 6.

1 _____
2 _____
3 _____
4 _____
5 _____

6 _____
7 _____
8 _____
9 _____
10 _____

8 Write comparative adjectives from Exercise 8 in the sentences. Make the sentences true for you.

1 I think studying medicine is _____ than business.
2 A nurse is usually _____ than a chef.
3 Working in an office is _____ than working in a store.
4 A scientist's job is _____ than a musician's.

PREPARING TO LISTEN

USING YOUR
KNOWLEDGE

UNDERSTANDING
KEY VOCABULARY

PRISM Online
Workbook

1 What is most important when you choose a new person for a job?

How the person is?
What the person knows?

2 Read the sentences and choose the best definition for the words in bold.

1 Robert is very **strong**. He can lift heavy things, so he is a good builder.
   a not physically powerful
   b physically powerful

2 Alissa is a very **kind** doctor. She cares a lot about her patients and wants them to feel good.
   a wanting to help others and show you care about them
   b very unpleasant and not friendly

3 Tomas is **polite**. He always says "please" and "thank you" to people.
   a behaving in a way that shows good manners and respect for others
   b shows bad manners and no respect for others

4 An engineer's job is a good **example** of a job that makes a lot of money.
   a something that is the opposite of what you are talking about
   b something that is typical of what you are talking about

5 Juan is **in shape** because he goes to the gym every day and eats healthy food.
   a healthy and strong, especially from exercising
   b not healthy and doesn't exercise

6 Alex wants to **teach** people how to cook.
   a to learn about new things
   b to give lessons at a school or university

3 You are going to listen to two managers choose someone for a job. Before you listen, read the job posting and answer the questions.

1 Where is the job?
2 What is the job?
3 What kind of person should apply?

About us

The UoY sports center is for students and staff at UoY. We have sports for men and women. We have a gym, a swimming pool, tennis courts, a soccer field, and a basketball court.

We have courses in yoga, pilates, zumba, kung-fu, running, cycling, swimming, and much more.

Fitness instructor
(Ref: UoY-SSv/SpC-0098)

The UoY sports center is looking for a new fitness instructor. We are looking for a person who:

- can teach sports and exercise.
- is friendly and helpful.
- has experience.

About you

You should:

- be strong and in shape.
- know three or more sports.
- speak English and French.

Click here to apply.

4 Work with a partner. Read about a person who wants the job. Then ask and answer the questions below.

Student A: Go to page 193.
Student B: Go to page 195.

1 Is it a man or a woman?
2 What's his / her name?
3 Where's he / she from?
4 What languages does he / she speak?
5 What sports can he / she teach?

5 Tell your partner about your person. Who should get the job?

Student A: Go to page 193.
Student B: Go to page 195.

WHILE LISTENING

LISTENING FOR
MAIN IDEAS

> **GLOSSARY**
>
> **experience** (n) knowledge that you get from doing a job

6 ▶ 5.6 Listen to two managers choose a new fitness instructor. Who do they choose, Alan or Lucy?

7 ▶ 5.6 Read the questions. Then listen again and circle the correct answers.

1 What other job do they talk about?
   a nurse
   b scientist
   c doctor

2 Paul thinks a good fitness instructor should
   a be strong and in shape.
   b be a good teacher.
   c teach tennis.

3 Paul likes Lucy because she's
   a a good scientist.
   b Canadian.
   c a fitness instructor.

4 Emma thinks a fitness instructor has to be
   a friendly and helpful.
   b strong and in shape.
   c kind and polite.

5 Emma thinks Alan can help students
   a work hard.
   b be polite.
   c have good ideas.

6 Paul thinks Lucy is better because she
   a has experience.
   b can teach popular sports.
   c can speak Cantonese.

DISCUSSION

8 Ask and answer the questions with a partner.

1 Do you agree with Paul? Why or why not?

2 What can happen in the workplace if managers choose the wrong person for a job?

3 Compare the jobs people talk about in Listening 1 and Listening 2. What experience do you need to have for the jobs? How is the experience for the jobs similar or different?

4 In both Listening 1 and Listening 2, people hear advice from others. Do the people follow the advice? Do you think they make the right decisions? Why or why not?

SPEAKING

CRITICAL THINKING

At the end of this unit, you are going to do the Speaking Task below.

> Choose a person for a job.

SKILLS

Understand criteria

Criteria are reasons for choosing something. Here are two examples from Listening 2:

I want a person who has experience—a person who can teach me tennis or volleyball.

We want a person who can make the students work hard.

▲ APPLY

1 Read about a job and answer the questions.

　1　What is the job?
　2　What are the job criteria?
　3　What kind of person do they want?

UNIVERSITY OF YUKON

Home

Jobs

Register for job ads

Manage job alerts

FAQ

Contact us

About us

Home > Jobs > **Current vacancies**

Sports Center Nurse (Ref: UoY-SSv/SpC-0099)
The UoY sports center is looking for a new nurse. We are looking for a person who has to:

- have experience in a hospital.
- speak another language.
- know about sports.
- be a hard worker.

About you
You should:

- be helpful.
- like sports.
- be friendly.

Click here to apply.

2 Work in a group of three. Read about a person who is applying for the nurse's job in the University of Yukon sports center. Take notes about your person.

Student A: Read about Inesh.
Student B: Read about Morena.
Student C: Read about Darren.

Student A

Home > Jobs > **Current vacancies**

About you

My name's Inesh, and I'm from Jakarta, Indonesia. I speak four languages: Indonesian, Chinese, Spanish, and English. I speak Spanish better than English.

I'm studying to be a nurse in a big hospital in Jakarta.

I'm polite and friendly. This is important because nurses have to help doctors and work with patients.

I would like to go to Canada and work in your sports center after I earn my degree.

Student B

Home > Jobs > **Current vacancies**

About you

My name's Morena, and I'm from São Paulo in Brazil. I speak Portuguese, Spanish, and English.

I'm a nurse in a small children's hospital. I like working with children, but I would like to work in your sports center in Canada.

I'm a friendly and helpful nurse. I love sports. I go running and do yoga. I'm strong and in shape. This is important because nurses have to work hard.

Student C

Home > Jobs > **Current vacancies**

About you

My name's Darren, and I'm from Chicago, Illinois, in the U.S. I'm a nurse in a big hospital. I work hard, and I'm good at my job.

I don't speak French, but I'm fast learner and a good student.

I'm healthy and in shape. I love soccer and basketball, and I go to a gym. This is important because a sports center nurse should play sports.

I would like to live in Canada.

3 Ask and answer the questions about the three people. Use the phrases to help you.

1 Where's he / she from?

He's / She's from ... in ...

2 What languages does he / she speak?

He / She speaks ...

He / She can't speak ...

3 Is he / she a student? (Where is he / she a student?)

Yes, he / she's a student in ...

No, he / she isn't.

4 Does he / she work in a hospital? (Where does he / she work?)

Yes, he / she works in ...

No, he / she doesn't.

5 What does he / she think is important?

He / She thinks it's important to ... because a nurse ...

▲ ANALYZE

4 Work in your group of three. Read the job criteria again. Who should be the new nurse? How does your person compare to the job criteria on page 118? Take notes.

person	job criteria

PREPARATION FOR SPEAKING

PRONUNCIATION FOR SPEAKING
WEAK SOUNDS IN COMPARATIVES

1 ▶ 5.7 Listen and repeat the comparative adjectives with the weak form /ər/.

> stronger   faster   harder   safer   kinder

COMPARING

2 Write words from the box to complete the sentences with information about Inesh, Morena, and Darren. Sometimes you need two words.

> better   bigger   experience   languages   more

1 Inesh speaks _____ _____ than Darren.
2 Morena and Darren have _____ _____ as nurses than Inesh.
3 Morena and Darren are _____ at sports than Inesh.
4 Darren works in a _____ hospital than Morena.

ASKING FOR AND GIVING OPINIONS AND REASONS

3 Look at the ways to ask for opinions and give opinions and reasons. Complete the dialogue with phrases in the box.

asking for opinions	giving opinions	giving reasons
What do you think about ... ?	I think that ... should be ...	Because he / she ...
Why do you think that?	I think that ...	Another reason is ...

A: What _____ think about Lucy?

B: I think that she _____ be the new fitness instructor.

A: Why _____ think that?

B: _____ she is a better teacher than Alan. Another _____ is the fitness instructor has to teach popular sports.

4 Work with a partner. Take turns asking for opinions, giving opinions, and giving reasons to choose the new nurse.

- Ask for opinions: What do you think about ... ?
  Why do you think that ... ?
- Give opinions: I think that ... should be the new nurse ...
  I think that he / she has to ...
- Give reasons: ... because he / she ... another reason is ...

SPEAKING TASK

Choose a person for a job.

PRISM Online Workbook

PREPARE

1 Review your notes comparing the person and job criteria in Critical Thinking.

2 Refer to the Task Checklist to prepare your discussion.

TASK CHECKLIST	✔
Use notes comparing your person to the nurse's job criteria.	
Ask for opinions, give opinions, and give reasons for your opinion.	
Use *should*, *have to*, and comparative adjectives.	
Use /ə/ to pronounce *have to* and *should*.	
Choose the new nurse.	

DISCUSS

3 Work in a small group. Decide who should be the new nurse.

4 Who is the new nurse? Tell the class your answer. Give opinions and reasons.

ON CAMPUS

ASKING POLITELY

PREPARING TO LISTEN

1 Read the situations. Who could you ask for help in each of these situations? Choose a person from the box.

1 Your sister is getting married, so you have to miss some classes: _____
2 You missed a class. You want information about the homework: _____
3 You need help with writing papers in English: _____

> **classmate** (n) a person in the same class as you
> **professor** (n) the person who teaches students at College or University
> **tutor** (n) the person who offers extra teaching to students at college or a university

2 Work with a partner and talk about the questions.

1 Which of the conversations in Exercise 1 are easy to have in English?
2 Which are more difficult?
3 Why are some conversations more difficult than others?

WHILE LISTENING

3 ▶ 5.8 You are going to listen to two of the situations from Exercise 1. Listen and write the situation number.

Conversation 1: _____   Conversation 2: _____

4 ▶ 5.8 Listen again and choose the correct answer.

1 Carla is asking permission to _____ .
   a go to Florida   **b** miss some classes
2 The professor says that Carla cannot _____ .
   a go to Florida   **b** miss any more classes
3 Selma wants to _____ .
   a work with a tutor   **b** work with her professor
4 Selma makes an appointment for Wednesday at _____ .
   a 10:30   **b** 12:15

Asking politely

It is important to use the right language when asking for permission or making a request.

Asking for permission	Making a request
May I please ... ?	Could you please ... ?
Could I ... ?	Can you ... ?
Is it possible to ... ?	

5 ▶ 5.8 Listen and complete the sentences with expressions from the box.

1 Professor, _____ speak to you for a moment?
   Yes, of course, Carla. What's up?

2 Please don't miss any more classes this semester.
   I won't.
   And, Carla ... _____ tell me again in a couple of weeks?

3 I can't come at that time. I have a class. _____ come later?
   Uh ... how about 12:15?

4 OK. Let's make it for 12:15. _____ give me your name?
   Yes, it's Selma ... S ... E ... L ... M ... A Chen. C ... H ... E ... N,

6 Look at the conversations in Exercise 5 again. Which ones show

1 someone asking permission?   2 someone making a request?

REAL-WORLD APPLICATION

7 Write what you would say in each of the situations.

1 You need your professor to repeat the instructions.
   _____ repeat the instructions?

2 You have to leave class early today.
   _____ leave class early today?

3 You need your classmate's email address.
   _____ give me your email address?

4 You need a copy of a handout.
   _____ give me a copy of the handout?

8 Work with a partner. Choose one of the situations below and act it out.

You have a job interview today. Ask your teacher if you can leave class early.

You do not understand the class. You think you need some help. Tell your teacher.

You missed two classes last week. Ask another student to tell you what you missed.

LEARNING OBJECTIVES

Listening skill	Listen for reasons
Pronunciation	Link words
Speaking skills	Ask for and give an opinion; agree and disagree
Speaking Task	Discuss ideas for a new café
On Campus	Participation and classroom behavior

HOMES AND BUILDINGS

ACTIVATE YOUR KNOWLEDGE

1 Look at the photo. Would you like to live here? Why or why not?

2 Would you like to visit this place? Why or why not?

3 What is special about this place?

PREPARING TO WATCH

ACTIVATING YOUR KNOWLEDGE

1 Work with a partner. Discuss the questions.

1 Do you prefer a small house or a large house? Why?
2 Do you prefer living in a big city or the country? Why?
3 Do you know the names of any famous houses?
4 Where do presidents of countries usually live?
5 Can you name any presidents of the United States?

PREDICTING CONTENT USING VISUALS

2 Look at the pictures from the video. Circle the correct answers.

1 The house is *large / long*.
2 The man is probably *important / modern*.
3 This room is probably a good place to *sleep / study*.
4 There are *no / many* gardens.

GLOSSARY

acre (n) a unit for measuring an outdoor area (1 acre = 0.4 hectare)

convenient (adj) easy to use, or suiting your plans well

Declaration of Independence (n) a very important piece of paper in U.S. history, signed on July 4, 1776

Native American (n) a member of the original groups of people who lived in North and South America

study (n) a room for reading and writing in a person's home

style (n) a way of doing something, especially one that is typical of a person, group of people, place, or time.

WHILE WATCHING

UNDERSTANDING MAIN IDEAS

3 ▶ Watch the video. Write *T* (true) or *F* (false) next to the statements. Correct the false statements.

_____ 1 Monticello was the home of Thomas Jefferson.
_____ 2 Jefferson was important to European history.
_____ 3 Monticello has many rooms.
_____ 4 The grounds around the house are not very large.

_____

_____

_____

_____

UNDERSTANDING DETAILS

4 ▶ Watch again. Fill in the blanks.

1 It took more than _____ years to build Monticello.
2 There are items from the New World (the U.S.A.) on the _____ in the Indian Hall.
3 A comfortable and _____ house was important for Jefferson.
4 Jefferson usually worked in his _____ in the morning.

5 Match the sentence halves.

MAKING INFERENCES

1 Monticello is
2 Jefferson did
3 Jefferson probably liked
4 Gardens and green spaces

a to hunt.
b were important to Jefferson.
c popular with American tourists.
d a lot of work at home.

DISCUSSION

6 Work with a partner. Discuss the questions.

1 Would you like to live in Monticello? Why or why not?
2 What's the most famous house in your city or country? Describe it.
3 Describe your dream home.

LISTENING

LISTENING 1

PREPARING TO LISTEN

1 Work with a partner. Ask and answer the questions.

1 What is your favorite restaurant? What do you like about it?
2 Is the way a restaurant looks as important as the food?
   Why or why not?

2 Write the words from the box to complete the sentences.

> **ceiling** (n) the top of a room that you can see when you look up
> **floor** (n) what you walk on inside a building
> **furniture** (n) things such as chairs, tables, and beds that you put in a home or office
> **room** (n) what the inside of a building is made up of
> **wall** (n) one of the sides of a room
> **wood** (n) the hard material that trees are made of

1 The painting on the _____ is fantastic. It looks like a photo!
2 The old, stone _____ is cold when you walk on it.
3 Look up at the _____ . It's painted to look like the sky!
4 Let's make the tables and chairs out of _____ . I like the color, and it smells like the forest.
5 We will need to buy more _____ so we have enough tables and chairs in the dining room.
6 We need a bigger _____ so we have space for all the new people and things for our business.

PRONUNCIATION FOR LISTENING

> **SKILLS**
>
> ### Linking words
>
> In English, you connect the end sound of a word with the beginning sound of the next word. This is called "linking words." Look at the how consonant sounds are linked to vowel sounds.
>
> Sandy Singh lives_in_India.
> Because_it's_a good_idea.

3 ▶ 6.1 Read the phrases from the interview. How do we pronounce the red and blue letters? Listen. Then circle the correct answer below.

1 an author of many books
2 I help architects.
3 For example
4 good ideas
5 restaurants in Los Angeles
6 What about the U.S.?

a We do not pronounce the red letters.
b We do not pronounce the blue letters.
c We pronounce the red and blue letters together.

WHILE LISTENING

LISTENING FOR
MAIN IDEAS

> **GLOSSARY**
>
> **architect** (n) someone who designs buildings
>
> **design** (n) the way something is planned and made
>
> **manage** (v) to be responsible for an office, shop, people, etc.
>
> **psychologist** (n) someone who knows about people's thoughts and feelings

4 ▶ 6.2 Listen to an interview on the radio. Circle the correct answers.

1 Dr. Thompson is ...
   a a psychologist.
   b an architect.
   c a restaurant manager.
2 Many Mexican restaurants have ...
   a orange walls.
   b red walls.
   c white walls.

3 Many Chinese restaurants have ...
   a orange walls and floors.
   b red walls and floors.
   c white walls and floors.
4 The main topic of the interview is ...
   a older buildings.
   b colors and feelings.
   c good food in restaurants.

Listening for reasons

Reasons are facts or opinions about why something happens. Reasons are important information. Speakers often use the words *why* and *because* to talk about reasons. Listen carefully when you hear the words *why* and *because*.

5 Match the reasons to the correct questions.

questions

1 Why is color important?
2 Why do many restaurants in Mexico have orange walls?
3 Why don't many restaurants in Los Angeles have orange walls?
4 Why do many Chinese restaurants have red walls?
5 Why is white a good color for an American restaurant?

reasons

a Because this is the color of fire and good things.
b Because it changes the way people think and feel.
c Because colors mean different things in different countries.
d Because this color makes people feel hungry.
e Because this color means fresh and clean.

6 ▶ 6.2 Listen again and check your answers.

DISCUSSION

7 Work with a partner. Ask and answer the questions.

1 What color would you use in a restaurant? Why?
2 What do some colors mean in your culture?
3 What is your favorite color? Why?

VOCABULARY FOR FURNITURE

1 ▶ 6.3 Listen to the words for the furniture in the photos. Repeat.

armchair

table

chair

bookcase

lamp

desk

sofa

2 Work with a partner. Take turns asking and answering the questions about the furniture in the photos. Write your answers in the table.

Would you have a ... (desk) in a café?

Would you have a ... (desk) in a home?

café	home
	desk

ADJECTIVES FOR FURNITURE

3 Look at the words in the box. They are adjectives used to describe furniture. Some words are both adjectives and nouns.

> **comfortable** (adj) Comfortable furniture and clothes make you feel relaxed.
>
> **glass** (adj, n) a hard, see-through material, used to make windows, bottles, etc.
>
> **leather** (adj, n) the skin of animals used to make things such as shoes and bags
>
> **metal** (adj, n) a hard, shiny material used to make knives and forks, bikes, and machines.
>
> **plastic** (adj, n) a material that can be made into different shapes, e.g. water bottles
>
> **uncomfortable** (adj) not feeling comfortable and pleasant
>
> **wooden** (adj) made of wood

4 ▶ 6.4 Listen and repeat the words.

5 Work with a partner. Take turns asking and answering the question to describe the furniture in Exercise 1.

What's this?   It's a ... comfortable armchair. / I'm not sure.

6 Write the adjectives you used to describe furniture in Exercise 5.

a _comfortable_ armchair   a _____ desk

a _____ table   a _____ bookcase

a _____ sofa   a _____ lamp

a _____ chair

LISTENING 2

PREPARING TO LISTEN

UNDERSTANDING
KEY VOCABULARY

PRISM Online Workbook

1 You are going to listen to two men discuss ideas for a new building. Before you listen, write the words from the box to complete the sentences.

> **cheap** (adj) not costing a lot of money
> **expensive** (adj) costing a lot of money
> **far** (adv) not close in location
> **modern** (adj) using the newest ideas, design, technology, etc.
> **near** (adv) very close in location
> **noisy** (adj) making a lot of noise
> **quiet** (adj) making little noise or no noise

1 This hotel costs a lot of money. It's very _____ .
2 The restaurant is very _____—people are talking and music is playing.
3 The library is _____ . There isn't much noise there, so we can study a bit better.
4 I like the new building! It's very _____ and looks really different and new.
5 You only have to walk a short way to the train station. It's _____ your building.
6 That place wouldn't be good because you have to drive 30 minutes or more to get there. It's too _____ from everything.
7 This hotel doesn't cost a lot of money. It's very _____ .

2 Work with a partner. Discuss your answers.

USING YOUR
KNOWLEDGE

1 Do you prefer modern or old buildings? Modern or old furniture?
2 Would you prefer a house in the city or the country? Why?

WHILE LISTENING

3 ▶ **6.5** Look at the map of a town. Then listen to two men discuss ideas for a new building and circle the correct answers.

1 What kind of building do they discuss?
  a a train station
  b a new office
  c a new hotel

2 Where is the new building going to be?
  a near the train station
  b downtown
  c near the park

3 Which of these statements is true?
  a They agree on every idea.
  b They agree on some ideas.
  c They don't agree on any ideas.

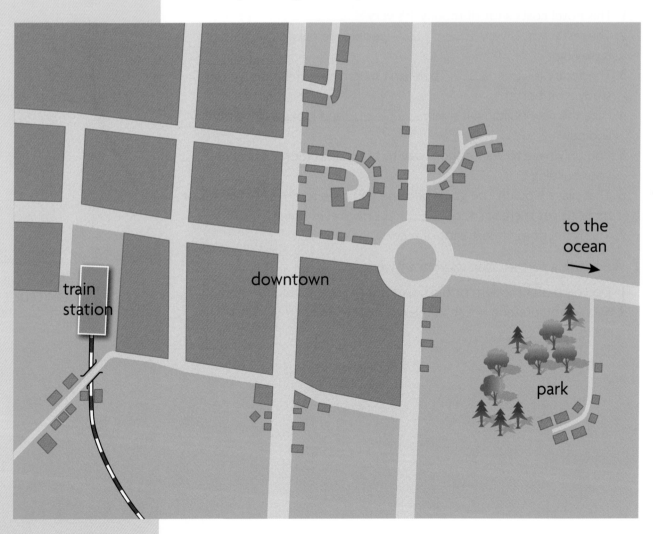

4 ▶ 6.5 Listen again. Circle the correct word.

1 The windows are going to be *big / small*.
2 The walls are going to be *blue / yellow*.
3 The desks are going to be made of metal and *wood / plastic*.
4 The chairs are going to be *plastic / comfortable*.

5 Work in groups. Compare your answers. Are they the same?

DISCUSSION

6 Work with a partner.

1 Do you agree with the two men? Why or why not?
2 Think of rooms where you study and work. What is the design? What is the color? How do you feel there? What would you change about the design?
3 Think about Listening 1 and Listening 2. Would you work with a psychologist to help you design a room or building? Why or why not?
4 Which do you think would be most important: the location, design, or color of a new space?

SPEAKING

CRITICAL THINKING

At the end of this unit, you are going to do the Speaking Task below.

> Discuss ideas for a new café.

ANALYZE

1 Look at photos of three cafés. Which café

    1 is noisy and downtown? _____

    2 has an expensive design with a lot of wood? _____

    3 is beautiful and quiet? _____

Café A

Café B

Café C

SKILLS

Find reasons for and against

Before you discuss something, find reasons for (positive) and against (negative) it. Record your ideas in a list or table to use during your discussion.

EVALUATE

2 You are going to open a new café. Find reasons for and against each type of café in the photos in Exercise 1. Then add them to the table. Use the sentences in the box to help you.

> It's expensive to eat there.   It's far away.
> It's easy to go there.   There are not many tables.
> It's popular with tourists.   It's expensive to build.
> You can't go there when the weather is bad.
> People can take beautiful photographs.
> It's an interesting building.

	+	−
Café A		
Café B		
Café C		

3 Look at the map of Green Town and read the information in the box below.

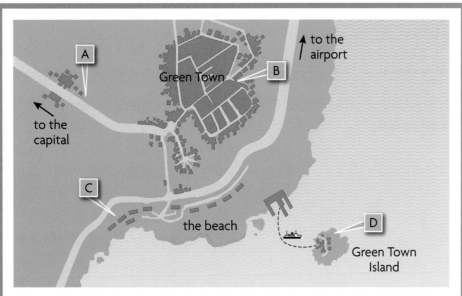

You are going to open a new café in Green Town. Green Town is a small town near the sea. There are two busy roads near the town. One road goes to the capital, and the other goes to the airport. Green Town is very popular with tourists. Tourists come from the capital and from countries around the world. There are ten big hotels on the beach. Green Town Island is also popular. Many tourists go on a day trip to the island. Other tourists stay in one of the island's three small hotels. Here are four places for your café:

A near the busy main road.
B in the town.
C on the beach.
D on Green Town Island.

4 Work in a group. Find reasons for and against each place on the map. Then add them to the table.

	+	−
A near the busy main road		
B in the town		
C on the beach		
D on Green Town Island		

5 Which kind of café (A, B, or C) would you like to open? Where would you like it to be?

PREPARATION FOR SPEAKING

REASONS, OPINIONS, AND AGREEMENT

1 ▶ 6.6 Listen to and read three parts of Listening 2. Notice the underlined phrases. Why do the people use them?

1

Dale: OK, so we need a place for our new office. <u>What about here</u>?

Hakan: Where?

Dale: Downtown. <u>What do you think</u>?

Hakan: Well, <u>it's a good place</u>. <u>It's near some good roads</u>. But … <u>I don't think we should go there</u>.

Dale: Oh? <u>Why not</u>?

Hakan: <u>Because the buildings downtown are very old</u>. <u>They are cold in winter and hot in summer</u>. <u>They're uncomfortable places</u>.

2

Dale: <u>What about here</u>?

Hakan: The park?

Dale: Yes. <u>It's quiet, and it's not far from a big road</u>. <u>What do you think</u>?

Hakan: Hmm, <u>I'm not sure</u>. <u>It's pretty far from the town</u>. <u>What about here</u>? Near the train station?

Dale: <u>The train station is good</u>. <u>It's good for travel</u> … but <u>I think we should go to the park</u>. <u>The buildings near the train station aren't cheap</u>.

3

Hakan: Now <u>what about the design</u>? <u>I think we should have a modern design with big windows</u>. <u>What about you</u>?

Dale: <u>Yes, I agree</u>. <u>Big windows are good</u>.

2 Write the underlined phrases in the correct column of the table.

give a reason	give an opinion	ask for an opinion	agree or disagree

GIVING REASONS

3 Look at the photos of the three cafés below. Which café would you like to go to? Why? Which café would you not like to go to? Why?
Use the phrases below to help you.

I would like to go to … because …
Another reason is that …
Also, it's … / it's not …
There is … there isn't … / There are … there aren't …
I wouldn't like to go to … because …

4 Stand up. Ask the questions in Exercise 3 to different students in the class.

Café A

Café B

Café C

GIVING AN OPINION

5 You are going to open a new school. Write four opinions. Use the phrases in the box to help you.

> have *big* / *small* classrooms
> have a *modern* / *traditional* building
> open the school in *a city* / *the country*
> have *computers* / *books* in class

I think we should have small classrooms.
1 I think we should _____ .
2 I think we should _____ .
3 I don't think we should _____ .
4 I don't think we should _____ .

ASKING FOR AN OPINION

6 Write the words from the box to complete the sentences.

blue   Mexican food   think   you

1 I like modern buildings. What about _____ ?
2 We want to paint the classroom. How about _____ ?
3 I'm going to open a new café. What do you _____ ?
4 Do you want to go to a restaurant this evening? How about _____ ?

AGREEING AND DISAGREEING

7 Do these sentences express agreement (A) or disagreement (D)?

1 I'm not sure.   _____
2 Yes, you're right.   _____
3 I don't agree.   _____
4 I agree.   _____

8 Work with a partner. Take turns being Student A and Student B.

Student A: Give an opinion from Exercise 5. Then ask for an opinion.
I think we should have big classrooms. What do you think?
I don't think we should have computers in class. What about you?

Student B: Agree or disagree with Student A.
Yes, I agree.
I'm not sure. I think we should have small classrooms.

PRISM Online Workbook

You are going to do the Speaking Task below.

Discuss ideas for a new café.

PREPARE

1 Look back at your notes in the tables in Critical Thinking. Use your notes and the phrases below to prepare your discussion.

- Where are you going to put your café?

What do you think?	It's near the sea.
What about … ?	There are a lot of hotels here.
I think we should go here.	It's near a busy road.
I think … is the best place.	There are a lot of people in the town.
Why?	Many tourists go on day trips to the island.
Because …	
Yes, I agree.	

- What kind of café is it going to be?

What about … ?	busy
How about … ?	comfortable
I think it should be a …	modern
Yes, I agree.	natural
	quiet
	traditional

- What kind of building is it going to be?

I think we should have	(a) big (a) small	window(s).		
The walls should be	metal.	blue.	brown.	
	plastic.	orange.	green.	
The tables and chairs should be	wooden.	red.	yellow.	
		white.		

2 Refer to the Task Checklist as you prepare for the discussion.

TASK CHECKLIST	✔
Discuss ideas for a café.	
Find reasons for and against.	
Ask for and give opinions.	
Prepare phrases for agreeing and disagreeing.	
Link consonant sounds with vowel sounds.	

DISCUSS

3 Work with a partner. Discuss your ideas for a new café.

Choose
- a place.
- a name.
- the design.

4 Tell the class your ideas.

ON CAMPUS

PARTICIPATION AND CLASSROOM BEHAVIOR

PREPARING TO LISTEN

1 Work with a partner. Look at the pictures. Who looks interested? Who looks bored? How do you know?

WHILE LISTENING

2 ▶ 6.7 Listen to the conversation. Why is the teacher talking to Sam?

3 ▶ 6.7 Listen to the conversation again. Write *T* (true) or *F* (false)

_____ **1** Sam does not like the class.
_____ **2** The class is difficult.
_____ **3** Sam was tired in class today.
_____ **4** Sam often looks at his cell phone in class.
_____ **5** The teacher thinks that Sam does not pay attention.
_____ **6** Sam asks a lot of questions in class.

4 Work in small groups. Discuss the questions.

1 Why does the teacher think Sam is not paying attention?
2 What does the teacher want Sam to do?

SKILLS

Participation and classroom behavior

Instructors and professors in North America expect students to actively participate in class. Classroom participation is often part of your final grade.

PRACTICE

5 How do you show that you are participating in class? Read the list below. Check (✔) the behaviors that are **usually**, **sometimes** or **never OK** to show participation.

	usually OK	sometimes OK	never OK
1 arriving late for class			
2 sleeping in class			
3 looking at the teacher when she / he is speaking			
4 asking questions in class			
5 looking at a cell phone in class			
6 asking the teacher to explain something again			
7 talking to another student			
8 leaving class early			
9 asking the teacher for help with an assignment			
10 doing other school work in class			

6 Work in small groups. Compare your answers. Do you agree?

REAL-WORLD APPLICATION

7 Work in small groups. Write some suggestions for international students on how to behave and not behave in a classroom in North America.

You should ...

1 _____

2 _____

3 _____

You should not ...

1 _____

2 _____

3 _____

8 Compare your answers with another group. Choose the best suggestions.

LEARNING OBJECTIVES

Listening skill	Listen for numbers
Pronunciation	Numbers with *-teen* and *-ty*; the letter *u*
Speaking skills	Introduce a report; talking about surveys
Speaking Task	Report the results of a survey
On Campus	Keeping healthy

FOOD AND CULTURE

ACTIVATE YOUR KNOWLEDGE

Work with a partner. Ask and answer the questions.

1 What can you see in the photo?

2 Do you often buy things like this?

3 Could this photo be from your country?

PREPARING TO WATCH

ACTIVATING YOUR KNOWLEDGE

1 Work with a partner. Discuss the questions.

1 What do children like to eat?
2 Do children eat lunch at school in your country?
3 What is a typical school lunch in your country?
4 What special or unusual food do people in your country eat?

PREDICTING CONTENT USING VISUALS

2 Look at the pictures from the video. Circle the correct answer

1 This city looks *busy / quiet*.
2 They children *catch / buy* their lunch.
3 The children eat *insects / chicken* for lunch.
4 The children are *happy / sad* at school.

GLOSSARY

habit (n) something that you regularly do

insect (n) a small creature with six legs, such as a bee or a fly

reporter (n) someone whose job is to find out and talk about news on TV, radio, or in a newspaper

---

WHILE WATCHING

3 Watch. Write *T* (true) or *F* (false) next to the statements below.

_____ 1 The reporter is in Thailand.

_____ 2 The students do not do homework, but they have to catch insects.

_____ 3 Students are eating insects for lunch.

_____ 4 It's unusual for the students to eat insects.

4 Watch again. Circle the correct answers.

1 The reporter is interested in _____ .
  a learning how to cook
  b teaching
  c food in other cultures

2 The school principal invited the reporter to _____ .
  a help cook lunch
  b teach a class
  c eat lunch

3 The insects are safe to eat because _____ .
  a they are strange
  b they are cooked in hot oil
  c they taste like potato chips

5 Match the sentence halves.

1 Eating insects is common	a think insects are an unusual food.
2 People eat foods	b in Thailand.
3 The students do not	c choose different food.
4 People in different cultures	d common in their culture.

DISCUSSION

6 Work with a partner. Discuss the questions.

1 What do people in your country usually eat for breakfast, lunch, and dinner?

2 What unusual animals do people around the world eat?

3 Is there a national food or meal in your country? Describe it.

LISTENING

LISTENING 1

PREPARING TO LISTEN

1 Work with a partner and discuss the questions.

1 What foods are popular in your culture?
2 How often do you eat
  • Chinese food?
  • Mexican food?
  • Italian food?
  • other kinds of food?

2 You are going to listen to part of a lecture about food and traditions. Before you listen, read the sentences. Write the words in bold next to the definitions.

1 **Meat** was very expensive in the past. Now, I eat beef and chicken often.
2 Growing **rice** is hard work, but millions of people eat it every day.
3 Today, in my city, there are many **international** foods. Mexican, Chinese, and Italian foods are very popular.
4 We eat a lot of **fish**. We live near water.
5 My grandmother makes many special **dishes**. She cooks all day to prepare them.
6 Salad is made of **vegetables**. It's very good for you. It's fresh and green.
7 I don't have time to cook dinner every night, so sometimes I eat **fast food**. But I know it's bad for me.

a _____ (n) food prepared in a special way and given a name
b _____ (n) parts of animals used as food
c _____ (n) small, white or brown grains from a plant that are cooked and eaten
d _____ (n) food that is served very quickly in a restaurant because it is already prepared
e _____ (n) plants that are used as food
f _____ (adj) from more than one country
g _____ (n) an animal that lives in water and swims using its tail and fins

PRONUNCIATION FOR LISTENING

Numbers with -teen and -ty

▶ 7.1 For -teen numbers (e.g., 13, 14, 15):

- stress the first syllable when the number is before a noun.
  Fif-teen thousand dollars every month?
  Se-ven-teen million?

- stress the last syllable when the number is at the end of a statement.
  Sorry—how many children? **Six-teen**?

For -ty numbers (e.g., 20, 30, 40), always stress the first syllable.
We feed **six-ty** children from poor families here. **Fif-ty**? No, **six-ty**.

PRISM Online Workbook

3 ▶ 7.2 Listen to and read these conversations. Circle the numbers you hear.

1. **A:** Is the number of people there about *17 / 70* million?
   B: Um, no, I think it's about *17 / 70*.
   A: *Seventeen / Seventy* million? OK, thanks.
2. **A:** We feed *16 / 60* children from poor families here.
   B: Sorry—how many children? *Sixteen / sixty*?
   A: No, *16 / 60*.
3. **A:** *Thirteen / Thirty* percent of this class are vegetarians—people who don't eat meat.
   B: *Thirteen / Thirty*? Are you sure?
   A: No, no—*13 / 30*!
4. **A:** People in this city eat *15 / 50* thousand tons of beef every month.
   B: Is that true? *Fifteen / Fifty* thousand tons every month?
   A: No, *15 / 50* thousand—not *15 / 50*.

WHILE LISTENING

LISTENING FOR
MAIN IDEAS

GLOSSARY

traditional (adj) doing things the way they have been done for a long time

4 ▶ 7.3 Listen to a lecture. What is the main topic of the lecture? Circle the correct answer.

a how our grandparents cooked traditional foods
b how more international foods are changing the way we eat
c how international foods are good for you

5 ▶ 7.3 Listen again. Write *T* (true) or *F* (false) for each statement.

_____ **1** Meat was always available in the U.S.

_____ **2** Raki's grandparents ate fish.

_____ **3** Jose's grandmother cooked traditional dishes.

_____ **4** International foods are available in Jose's country.

_____ **5** Most of the students know how to cook traditional dishes.

Listening for numbers

You often hear facts in lectures. Many facts are about numbers.

There are **40** students in the class.

In Argentina, **97%** of the people can read and write.

PRISM Online Workbook

6 ▶ 7.3 Listen again. Write the number you hear next to each phrase.

1 _____ = how many times Americans eat meat every year

2 _____ years ago = how long ago Jose's grandmother cooked traditional food every day

3 _____ = the number of students who can cook

4 _____ percent = the number of students who can cook traditional foods

7 Work with a partner. Compare answers. Use the phrases below to help you.

What do you have for number ... ?

I have ...

What about you?

I don't know the answer.

DISCUSSION

8 Work in groups. Discuss the questions.

1 What foods did your family eat when you were a child? What do you eat now?

2 Do you think it's important to know how to cook traditional food? Why or why not?

3 Are there some foods people in your country do not eat? Why or why not?

THE SIMPLE PAST 1

Statements

Use the simple past to talk about an event or an activity in the past.

Add -ed to most regular verbs in the past or just -d to verbs that end in -e.

My grandmother **cooked** *traditional dishes.*

We **lived** *in a big city 10 years ago.*

subject	verb + -ed
I / He / She / You / We / They	cooked dinner last night.

Add *did + not / didn't* before the base form of the verb in the negative.

My grandmother **didn't cook** *traditional dishes.*

We **didn't live** *in a big city 10 years ago.*

subject	did not / didn't + base form of the verb
I / He / She / You / We / They	**did not cook** traditional dishes. **didn't cook** traditional dishes.

PRISM Online Workbook

1 Write the verb in the simple past.

1 We _____ (live) in Mexico 10 years ago.

2 My mom _____ (cook) Italian food a lot.

3 I _____ (not cook) last night.

4 My grandfather _____ (work) in a restaurant.

Yes/No questions and short answers

Use *did* or *didn't* + subject + base form of the verb to form questions in the simple past.

did / didn't	subject	base form of the verb
Did	you	eat dinner last night?
Didn't	you	eat dinner last night?

Short answers:

Yes, I did.   No, I didn't.

2 Answer the questions so they are true for you.

1 When you were a child, did you live in a big city?
   No, I didn't live in a big city. I lived in a small town.

2 Did both of your parents work?

   _____

3 Did your grandmother cook traditional dishes?

   _____

4 Did you celebrate holidays with special foods?

   _____

5 Did your family talk a lot at the dinner table?

   _____

6 Did you watch TV during dinner?

   _____

3 Write the questions in the simple past. Then work with a partner and ask and answer the questions.

1 have a traditional meal last night?
   Did you have a traditional meal last night?

2 eat at a fast food restaurant this week?

   _____

3 cook dinner last week?

   _____

4 not eat lunch yesterday?

   _____

4 Work with a new partner. Ask and answer the questions about your old partner.

LANGUAGE

Irregular verbs

Some verbs are irregular. They do not add -d / -ed in the simple past.

be → was / were	go → went
buy → bought	have → had
come → came	make → made
do → did	read → read
eat → ate	

I **made** a special dish from my country last week.
I **ate** something new last night.
This vegetable **came** from Mexico.

Remember: Use the base form after *didn't* in the negative.
I **didn't eat** dinner last night.

5 Write the verbs in the simple past.

1 No, I _____ (not make) special dishes for the party.
2 He _____ (eat) a lot of fish in Japan.
3 She _____ (buy) a lot of food at the supermarket.
4 No, it _____ (be) too expensive, so people didn't eat it very much.
5 No, she _____ (not do) any cooking when she was visiting her family.
6 This vegetable _____ (come) from South America.
7 We _____ (not have) time to cook last night, so we _____ (go) to a restaurant.
8 I _____ (read) an interesting cookbook about Mexican food last night.

VOCABULARY FOR FOOD

6 Look at the photos of different kinds of food. Add as many foods to the chart as you can.

meat	vegetables	other

7 Work with a partner. Are the photos of fast food (*F*), traditional food (*T*), or healthy food (*H*)? Write *F*, *T*, or *H* under to the photos. More than one letter is possible.

1 _____

2 _____

3 _____

4 _____

5 _____

6 _____

7 _____

8 _____

8 How many students in the class like each kind of food? Stand up and ask and answer questions. Use the phrases from the box to help you.

questions	Do you like ... ?
	What about ... ?
	What food don't you like?
	What's the food you like best?
	Is this a traditional food in your country? Which foods do you use to make a traditional dish in your country?
answers	I like ... because ... I don't like ... because ...
	The food I like best is ...
	Yes / No ...
	In my country, we use ... to make ...

LISTENING 2

PREPARING TO LISTEN

UNDERSTANDING
KEY VOCABULARY

PRISM Online Workbook

1 Write the words from the box to complete the sentences.

> **culture** (n) the usual way of living in a country or for a group of people
> **enjoy** (v) to get pleasure from something
> **favorite** (adj) your favorite person or thing is the one you like best
> **healthy** (adj) good for your health
> **home-cooked** (adj) food cooked at home
> **meal** (n) the food that you eat at breakfast, lunch, or dinner

1 My grandmother almost never ate at restaurants. She always made good food at home. Everyone liked her _____ food.
2 Which _____ do you like the best—breakfast, lunch, or dinner?
3 Eating out is not always _____ . It's probably better to cook fresh food at home.
4 My _____ food is Italian.
5 I really _____ going to restaurants that serve international food. It's always fun to try something new.
6 In my country's _____ , we usually make special meals for celebrations and holidays.

2 You are going to hear a student give a report. Before you listen, look at the information below.

1 What kind of restaurant are you going to hear about in Question 1?
2 Which answer do you think will be more popular to Question 2: "Yes" or "No"?
3 What do you think the answer will be in Question 3?

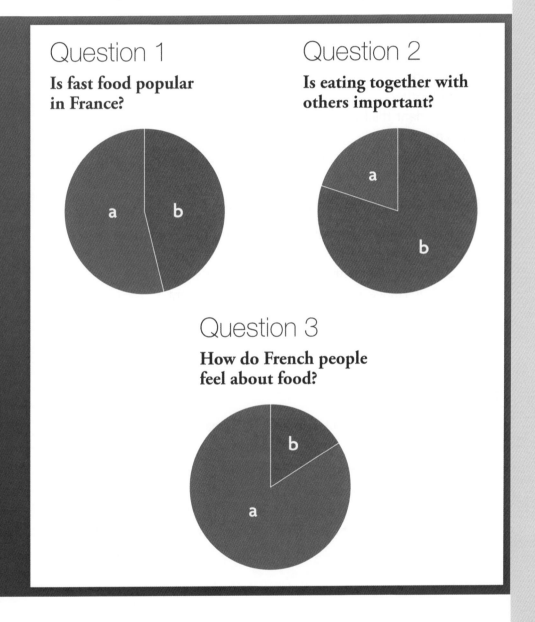

Question 1

Is fast food popular in France?

Question 2

Is eating together with others important?

Question 3

How do French people feel about food?

WHILE LISTENING

3 ▶ 7.4 Listen to a student report the results of a survey. Circle the correct answers.

1 The main topic of her survey is
   a food from around the world.
   b food and culture in one country.
   c family meals.
2 Most people eat meals
   a alone.
   b at work.
   c with others.
3 The student thinks that fast food
   a is not popular.
   b is changing the way people eat in France.
   c tastes bad in France.

4 ▶ 7.4 Listen again. Write *T* (true) or *F* (false) for each statement.

_____ 1 Fifty-four percent of all restaurant sales were from fast food places.
_____ 2 Eighty percent of people like to eat with others.
_____ 3 In France, enjoying food is very important.
_____ 4 Because of the French culture, fast food restaurants have to cook better meals than usual.
_____ 5 Traditions about eating are the same now as they were before.

DISCUSSION

5 Work with a partner. Think about the information from Listening 1 and Listening 2 and talk about the questions.

1 How do people feel about food in your country?
2 Is fast food more popular than home-cooked meals in your country?
3 How is your culture changing because of foods from other countries?
4 Should countries not allow so many foods from other countries? Why or why not?

SPEAKING

CRITICAL THINKING

At the end of this unit, you are going to do the Speaking Task below.

Report the results of a survey.

> **SKILLS**
>
> ### Using pie charts
>
> The diagrams in Listening 2 on page 159 and below are pie charts. We can use pie charts to show results from a survey in a different way from just numbers. Pie charts use percentages (%).

1 ▶ **7.4** Work with a partner. Use the words from the box to label parts a and b in the diagrams on page 159. Then listen again and check.

> fast food sales / sales from other restaurants
> eating together is important / eating together is not important
> enjoy food / don't enjoy food

2 Work in two groups, A and B. Look at the information in your pie charts.

APPLY ▲

Group A: Changes in food and culture—country A

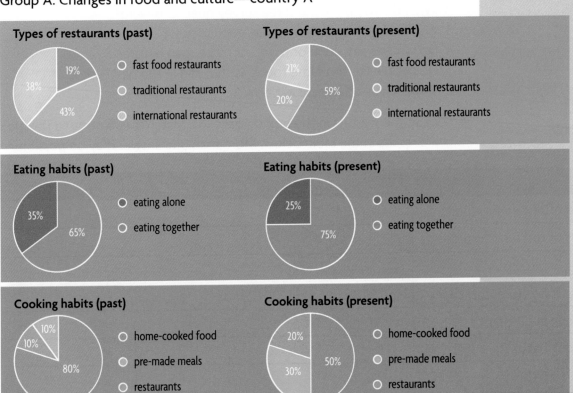

Types of restaurants (past)

19%
38%
43%

- ○ fast food restaurants
- ○ traditional restaurants
- ● international restaurants

Types of restaurants (present)

21%
59%
20%

- ○ fast food restaurants
- ○ traditional restaurants
- ○ international restaurants

Eating habits (past)

35%
65%

- ○ eating alone
- ○ eating together

Eating habits (present)

25%
75%

- ○ eating alone
- ○ eating together

Cooking habits (past)

10%
10%
80%

- ○ home-cooked food
- ○ pre-made meals
- ○ restaurants

Cooking habits (present)

20%
50%
30%

- ○ home-cooked food
- ○ pre-made meals
- ○ restaurants

Group B: Changes in food and culture—country B

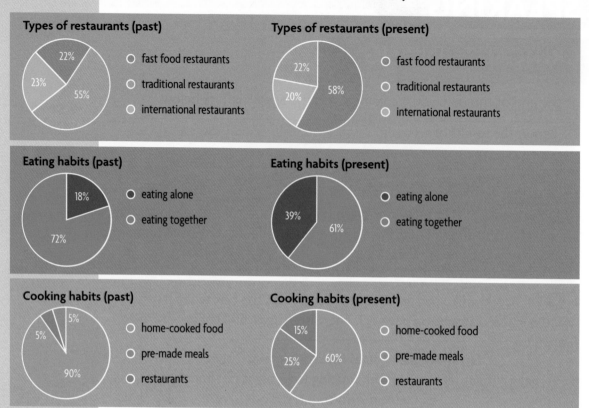

Types of restaurants (past)

22%
23%
55%

○ fast food restaurants
○ traditional restaurants
○ international restaurants

Types of restaurants (present)

22%
20%
58%

○ fast food restaurants
○ traditional restaurants
○ international restaurants

Eating habits (past)

18%
72%

○ eating alone
○ eating together

Eating habits (present)

39%
61%

○ eating alone
○ eating together

Cooking habits (past)

5%
5%
90%

○ home-cooked food
○ pre-made meals
○ restaurants

Cooking habits (present)

15%
25%
60%

○ home-cooked food
○ pre-made meals
○ restaurants

3 Work in your groups and answer the questions.

1 What information does each pie chart show?
2 What do you think the three survey questions were?
3 Are fast food restaurants more popular now?
4 Do families eat alone or together more than before?
5 Do people eat the same foods as they did in the past?
6 What foods do people eat now?

🔺 ANALYZE

4 Look at the reasons in the box on page 163. Match the reasons to the pie chart results in the table below. More than one answer may be possible.

pie chart	reason for result
Types of restaurants (past)	
Types of restaurants (present)	
Eating habits (past)	
Eating habits (present)	
Cooking habits (past)	
Cooking habits (present)	

People eat smaller lunches, such as fast food, which don't take as long.

Families are not together because of work hours.

Families eat at popular fast food restaurants as a special occasion.

Families ate big lunches together.

More foods are available from around the world.

Fast food is cheap and easy.

People don't know how to cook.

Pre-made meals are available at supermarkets.

Traditional restaurants are more expensive.

International foods or international restaurants are more popular.

Fast food was not available.

People couldn't buy foods from other countries.

People don't have time to cook.

5 Think of other reasons for the results in the pie charts and add them to the chart. Use Listening 1 and Listening 2 to help you.

PREPARATION FOR SPEAKING

INTRODUCING A REPORT

1 ▶ 7.5 Sophie uses six statements to introduce paragraphs in her report. Number the statements in the correct order. Then listen and check.

_____ **a** My questions were on the topic of food and culture in France.

_____ **b** This afternoon, I'm going to tell you about the results of my survey.

_____ **c** There were three questions in my survey.

_____ **d** I'm Sophie.

_____ **e** I think this is an interesting topic.

_____ **f** Hello!

2 ▶ 7.6 Listen to two more introductions. Write the words from the box in the spaces below.

> three   five   everybody   fast   good
> interesting   morning   traditional

> Good (1)_____ ! I'm Tomoko. I'm going to tell you about the results of my survey. There were (2)_____ questions in my survey. My topic was (3)_____ Japanese food. I think this is an (4)_____ topic.

> Hello, (5)_____ ! I'm Ahmed. I'm going to tell you about the results of my survey. My topic was (6)_____ food in Abu Dhabi. There were (7)_____ questions in my survey. I think this is a (8)_____ topic.

PRONUNCIATION FOR SPEAKING

SKILLS

The letter *u*

The letter *u* is pronounced in different ways. Look at the words with different *u* sounds below.

> question   survey   result   U.S   popular

3 ▶ 7.7 Listen to the different *u* sounds in the words in the box. Then, listen again and repeat.

4 ▶ 7.8 Listen to the sentences with the *u* sound underlined.
Listen again and repeat.

1 I'm going to tell you about the <u>results</u> of my <u>survey</u>.
2 There were <u>four</u> <u>questions</u> about food and <u>culture</u>.
3 Are fast food restaurants <u>popular</u>?
4 People had 80 <u>minutes</u> for <u>lunch</u>.

TALKING ABOUT SURVEYS

5 ▶ 7.9 Listen to six statements from Sophie's report.

a My last question was
b my second question was
c So, when you look here,
d In one survey I read,
e You can see here that
f my first question was

6 ▶ 7.9 Write the correct phrases in the spaces in the statements.
Listen and check.

1 So, _____ , "Do they eat a lot of fast food in France?"
2 _____ 54% percent of all restaurant sales were from fast food places.
3 _____ , in the past, people had 80 minutes for lunch and now, only 22 minutes.
4 _____ "Is eating together with others important?"
5 _____ , "How do the French feel about food?"
6 _____ , 84% of the people in France enjoy food.

7 Work with a partner. Take turns reporting on the survey questions about food and culture in country A and country B from Critical Thinking. Use the phrases in Exercise 5 to talk about the pie charts.

My first question was, "Are fast food restaurants popular
now?" You can see here that the answer is "yes." In the past,
_____ % of all restaurants were fast food restaurants.
Now, _____ % of the restaurants are fast food restaurants.

Report the results of a survey.

PREPARE

1 Work with a partner. One student is from Group A (country A) in Critical Thinking. The other student is from Group B (country B).

2 Review the results of the survey about country A or country B and your answers and reasons to the questions in Critical Thinking.

3 Prepare an introduction for your report.

Hello, _____ ! I'm _____ .
I'm going to tell you about the results of a survey. The topic
was _____ in (country A / B). There were
_____ questions in the survey. I think this is a / an
_____ topic.

4 Refer to the Task Checklist below as you prepare your report.

TASK CHECKLIST	✔
Report the results of the survey about country A or B.	
Use your answers and reasons to the three survey questions in your report.	
Introduce your report.	
Use the pie charts in your report.	
Use the correct stress and -teen / -ty pronunciation for numbers. Use the correct pronunciation for the u sound.	

DISCUSS

5 Talk about the results from the survey about your country. Use your notes from Critical Thinking. Practice your introduction.

6 Change partners and report the results of your survey.

ON CAMPUS

KEEPING HEALTHY

PREPARING TO LISTEN

1 You are going to listen to two students talking about their lifestyles. Before you listen, discuss the questions with a partner.

1 Which pictures show a healthy lifestyle? Which do not?
2 How can students keep healthy on campus?
3 What do you think about the advice in the box?

IF YOU WANT TO SUCCEED IN COLLEGE, YOU NEED TO KEEP YOUR BODY HEALTHY. THIS MEANS:

eating healthy food   exercising regularly   getting enough sleep

WHILE LISTENING

2 ▶ 7.10 Listen to Kelly and Mark describe their lifestyles.

3 ▶ 7.10 Listen again and check (✔) the boxes.

Who ...	Kelly	Mark
1 eats hamburgers and pizza?		
2 eats a lot of vegetables?		
3 gets regular exercise?		
4 drinks energy drinks?		
5 drinks water?		
6 goes to bed early?		
7 goes to bed late?		

4 Work with a partner. Compare your answers to Exercise 3. Which student has the healthier lifestyle? Why? Which student is more like you?

PRACTICE

5 Here are some guidelines for students to stay healthy. Match the sentence halves.

1 Try to go to sleep _____
2 If you want to exercise regularly, _____
3 Begin every day _____
4 Half of your plate should be _____
5 Drink water instead of _____
6 Salad is good, but _____
7 When you buy packaged food, _____

a with a healthy breakfast.
b check the ingredients for sugar and salt.
c do something that you enjoy.
d at the same time every night.
e don't use too much salad dressing.
f vegetables.
g coffee or energy drinks.

6 Work in small groups. Do you agree with the guidelines? Why?

REAL-WORLD APPLICATION

7 You are going to interview your classmates about healthy lifestyles. Work in pairs. Write five more questions about the topics in the box.

> exercise   sleep habits   cooking and eating
> fast food   snacks   drinks

1 How often do you exercise? _____
2 _____
3 _____
4 _____
5 _____
6 _____

8 Ask another pair your questions and answer their questions.

9 Discuss the questions below.

1 Do you have a healthy lifestyle?
2 What do you find difficult about having a healthy lifestyle?
3 What advice would you give students about how to stay healthy?

LEARNING OBJECTIVES

Listening skill	Synthesize information
Pronunciation	Years; *-d* / *-ed* endings in regular simple past verbs
Speaking skills	Describe a topic; describe a problem; describe a solution; describe results
Speaking Task	Describe a transportation problem, solutions, and results
On Campus	Find help

TRANSPORTATION

ACTIVATE YOUR KNOWLEDGE

Work with a partner. Ask and answer the questions.

1 Which country do you think is shown in the photo? Why?

2 Which forms of transportation in the photo

   a are more modern?

   b did people use in the past?

3 Do you think this city has a problem with transportation?

WATCH AND LISTEN

PREPARING TO WATCH

ACTIVATING YOUR KNOWLEDGE

1 Work with a partner. Discuss the questions.

1 How do you get to school?
2 Are the roads busy? Is there a lot of traffic?
3 Are the roads big and wide or small and narrow in your town or city?

PREDICTING CONTENT USING VISUALS

2 Look at the pictures from the video. Put the words in order to make sentences.

1 many roads / has / The / city / .

_____

2 not much traffic / There is / in / the country / .

_____

3 The road / the mountain / goes / under/ .

_____

4 bridge / long / The / is / .

_____

GLOSSARY

amazing (adj) very surprising

connect (v) to join two things together

construct (v) to build, for example, houses or roads

highway (n) a main, usually large, road

port (n) an area of a town next to water where ships arrive and leave

WHILE WATCHING

3 ▶ Watch the video. Write *T* (true) or *F* (false) next to the statements below. Correct the false statements.

_____ 1 More people travel on roads today.

_____ 2 The largest builder of roads is in the United States.

_____ 3 China has 47,000 miles of highways.

_____ 4 The G50 connects the middle of China to Shanghai.

_____ 5 The Sidu Bridge is not the world's highest bridge.

_____

_____

_____

_____

4 ▶ Watch again. Put the sentences in the order that you hear them.

_____ In 1989 China had fewer than 100 miles of highway.

_____ The G50 goes through mountains, and includes the largest bridge.

_____ The G50 is 1,200 miles long.

_____ The number of roads is growing all the time.

_____ China has more highways than the United States.

5 Circle the correct answer. Compare your answers with a partner.

1 Why does China need more roads?
   a There are more people visiting China.
   b The country is growing.
   c There are many old roads.

2 Why is it important to connect the middle of China to the port city of Shanghai?
   a People in the middle of China want to travel to Shanghai.
   b People like to visit the east coast.
   c People in the middle of China can easily send and receive more things.

DISCUSSION

6 Work with a partner. Discuss the questions.

1 Is your city or country building more roads every year? Why or why not?

2 What important places do the main roads in your country connect?

3 Is there a road similar to the G50 in your country? What is it?

4 Do you think the G50 is amazing? Why?

LISTENING

PREPARING TO LISTEN

UNDERSTANDING
KEY VOCABULARY

1 Write the words from the box to complete the sentences.

> **bus** (n) a big type of car that takes many people around a city
> **passenger** (n) someone who travels in a car, bus, etc., but doesn't drive it
> **subway** (n) trains that travel underground, usually in a city
> **taxi** (n) a car with a driver who you pay to take you somewhere
> **ticket** (n) a small piece of paper that shows you paid to do something
> **train** (n) a long, thin type of car that travels on metal tracks and carries people or things
> **travel** (v) to go from one place to another, usually over a long distance
> **trip** (n) when you go to a place for a short time and come back again

1 I'm only going for two days. It's a short _____ .
2 My children take the _____ to school every day. It stops on our street. The driver is very nice and knows everyone's name.
3 I'm sorry, but there is no public transportation here. I can call a _____ to take you to the airport from your hotel. It will cost about $60.
4 The _____ is one of the best in the world. It's fast and easy to use. Millions of people use it every day.
5 When I was in Europe, I rode on the _____ from city to city. It was a great way to see the countryside and small towns.
6 There was a nice _____ who gave me his seat because it was the only one free.
7 Excuse me. I would like to go to Hanover Station. How much is a one-way _____ , please?
8 In many cities, people _____ many miles to work.

2 Work with a partner and discuss your answers.

1 What do you know about London?

2 How do you think people travel to work and school in London?

3 Circle the correct word in each sentence.

1 Excuse me! How much is a train *passenger* / *ticket* to Liverpool?

2 Hi! How was your *trip* / *passenger* to London?

3 I had a conversation with an interesting *passenger* / *ticket* on the train.

4 You are going to listen to a man named Steve Miller talk about transportation for London. Before you listen, decide if the types of transportation in the box are private (only for the person who owns it) or public (for everyone to use). Write them in the correct column of the table.

> bus   car   subway   taxi   train

private	public

5 What types of transportation do you think are in London?

PRONUNCIATION FOR LISTENING

SKILLS

Pronouncing years

Pronounce years in two parts with *and* or two parts only.

1994	[nineteen] [ninety-four]
1238	[twelve] [thirty-eight]
570	[five hundred] and [seventy] / [five hundred seventy]
2005	[two thousand] and [five] / [two thousand five]
2017	[two thousand] and [seventeen] / [two thousand seventeen] or [twenty seventeen]

6 ▶ 8.1 Look at the years. Listen and repeat.

| 1238 | 1868 | 1923 | 1996 | 2005 |

7 ▶ 8.2 Listen and write the years.

1 _____   3 _____   5 _____

2 _____   4 _____

8 How is the last number in Exercise 7 different?

PREDICTING CONTENT USING VISUALS

> **GLOSSARY**
>
> **result** (n) something that happens because something else has happened

9 Work with a partner. What can you see in the photos?

a the London Underground—the world's oldest subway system

b Steve Miller works for Transport for London.

c There are many people who travel in London.

d Many Londoners use an electronic ticket, the Oyster card.

e an electronic gate from the London Underground

WHILE LISTENING

10 ▶ 8.3 Listen to Steve Miller talk about Transport for London and take notes.

Topic: (1)_____

Transport for London: (2)_____
_____

People traveling in London: (3)_____
_____

London Underground opened: (4)_____

Oyster card:
(5)_____

11 Work with a partner. Use your notes to answer the questions.

1 What is the topic of Steve's talk?
2 What does Transport for London (TfL) do?
3 How many people travel in London?
4 What's the age of the London Underground?
5 What is an Oyster card?

12 ▶ 8.3 Listen again and answer the questions.

1 Which five forms of transportation does Steve talk about?
- London Underground
- _____
- _____
- _____
- _____

2 What year did TfL introduce Oyster cards?
3 Why did TfL need Oyster cards?

DISCUSSION

13 Work with a partner. Ask and answer the questions.

1 Do you live in a busy city? If not, have you visited one? Do / Did you like it?
2 Which types of transportation do you use? What do you use them for?
3 Which type of transportation do you use most often? Why?

VERBS FOR TRANSPORTATION

take a bus, train, subway, taxi

bus

train

subway

taxi

drive a car

car

go by bus, train, subway, taxi, car

bus

train

car

subway

taxi

ride a bike

bicycle / bike

ride a motorcycle

motorcycle

go on foot

foot

1 Write the correct form of the verbs. Use the chart with verbs for transportation to help you.

   1 Can you _____ a bike?
   2 Can you _____ a subway to the supermarket in your hometown?
   3 Do you like to _____ by train or by bus?
   4 Do you know how to _____ a car?
   5 Where do you _____ on foot?

2 Respond to the questions in Exercise 1 with answers that are true for you. Then work with a partner and practice asking and answering the questions.

   1 Yes, I can ride a bike. / No, I can't ride a bike.

THE SIMPLE PAST 2

More irregular verbs

Use the simple past to talk about an event or activity in the past.
There are many irregular past tense verbs. They do not add -d / -ed in the simple past. You learned some irregular past tense forms in Unit 7. Here are more irregular verbs in the simple past.

drive → drove
go → went
ride → rode
run → ran
sit → sat
take → took

3 Write the verbs in parentheses in the simple past.

   1 It was raining. She _____ (take) a taxi.
   2 He _____ (run) to the train station.
   3 She _____ (sit) by the window.
   4 They _____ (ride) bikes.
   5 She _____ (drive) to her friend's house.
   6 She _____ (go) by bus.

BECAUSE / SO

Use *because* and *so* to show reasons why something happened or the result of something. *Because* and *so* are followed by a subject and verb.

Because + subject and verb: to show a reason
So + subject and verb: to show a result

I took the train **because** it was faster. (reason: **because** it was faster)
It was a beautiful day, **so** I rode my bike. (result: **so** I rode my bike)

PRISM Online Workbook

4 Match the sentences from Exercise 3 to the reasons and results using *because* and *so*. Then write the complete sentences.

_____ **a** ... because he was late.
   He ran to the train station because he was late.

_____ **b** ... because it was too far to walk.
   _____

_____ **c** ... so she could see the beautiful countryside.
   _____

_____ **d** ... so as not to get wet from the rain.
   _____

_____ **e** ... because there was a bus station near her house.
   _____

_____ **f** ... because it was good exercise and didn't use gas.
   _____

5 Work with a partner. Write information that is true for you.

1 I like to go on foot because ... / I don't like to go on foot because ...
2 I ride a bike because ... / I don't ride a bike because ...
3 I like to go by train, so ... / I don't like to go by train, so ...
4 Gas is expensive, so ... / Gas isn't expensive, so ...

PREPARING TO LISTEN

USING YOUR
KNOWLEDGE

1 You are going to listen to someone describe a solution to a transportation problem. Before you listen, look at the pictures and discuss the questions with a partner.

traffic

moving sidewalk

carpooling

pollution

self-driving car

1 Which of these things in the pictures do you have in your country?
2 How do you feel about what you see in the pictures?

2 Write the words from the box to complete the sentences.

UNDERSTANDING
KEY VOCABULARY

---

accident (n) a situation that causes pain or problems
bike (n) a type of transportation with two wheels that you sit on and move by turning two pedals (= parts you press with your feet)
gas (n) what cars need in order to drive
idea (n) a suggestion or plan for doing something
problem (n) something that makes life difficult and needs a solution
sidewalk (n) a hard path for people to walk on next to a road
traffic (n) the cars, trucks, etc. driving on the road

---

1 The city had a new _____ to make travel times shorter for people.
2 There are too many cars and trucks on the road. The _____ is very bad today!
3 Oh, dear. I have to put more _____ in my car before I go to work. It's so expensive!
4 We need more roads or buses or subways. It's a big _____ in many big cities.
5 I like to ride my _____ to work. It's great exercise!
6 There was an _____ on this road last night, and people were hurt.
7 It's too hot outside in this city, so people don't like to walk on the _____ .

PRISM Online Workbook

WHILE LISTENING

3 ▶ 8.4 Listen to someone describe a solution to a transportation problem and take notes. Then compare your notes with a partner.

Topic: (1)_____

Facts:

Cities have a lot of (2)_____ problems. Many people use their
(3)_____.

It takes more (4)_____ and (5)_____ to
travel around the city.

This is (6)_____ for people, and the (7)_____
is very bad.

Solutions:

Some cities think that (8)_____ are a good idea.

Other cities have (9)_____.

There's another new (10)_____ that is interesting.

It's a (11)_____ car!

It can help stop (12)_____.

Dubai

Problem:

(13)_____

_____

Solution:

(14)_____

Result:

(15)_____

Problem:

(16)_____

_____

Solution:

(17)_____

Results:

(18)_____

4 Answer the questions. Use your notes to help you.

1 Why do cities have traffic problems?
2 What are some problems with cars?
3 What do some cities think are good ideas?
4 Which place is working hard to improve their traffic problems?
5 What is the plan in this place?

DISCUSSION

Synthesizing information

When you *synthesize information*, you mix information from one source (e.g., a text or a listening) with information from another source. It helps you to understand problems, explain results, or find a solution.

5 Work with a partner. Discuss the questions. Use the information from Listening 1 and Listening 2 to help you.

SYNTHESIZING

1 In Listening 1, you hear about the London Underground. In Listening 2, Dubai plans to build a subway like London's. Do you think people in Dubai will use the subway as much as people do in London? Why or why not?

2 In Dubai, inside sidewalks are a solution to a transportation problem. Do you think there should be inside sidewalks in London? Why or why not? What are some other cities where inside sidewalks would help?

3 How are transportation problems the same in London and Dubai? How are they different?

4 Do you think that public transportation is always a good solution? Why or why not?

SPEAKING

CRITICAL THINKING

At the end of this unit, you are going to do the Speaking Task below.

Describe a transportation problem, a solution, and result.

▲ REMEMBER

1 Write down the transportation problems, solutions, and results you heard in Listening 1 and Listening 2 in the chart. Use your notes to help you.

problem	solution	result
paper tickets very slow	Oyster cards / credit cards	pay online / walk through gates faster

2 Work in two groups.
Group A: Go to page 193 and read about the transportation problems, their solutions, and the results in Mexico City, Santa Fe District, Mexico. Then answer the questions.
Group B: Go to page 195 and read about the transportation problems, their solutions, and the results in Los Angeles, California, U.S.A. Then answer the questions.

SKILLS

Synthesizing and organizing information

For your talk, you will use information from this unit, from your discussions, and from your own ideas, which you will synthesize and organize.

▲ UNDERSTAND

3 **Group A:** Complete the chart with your answers from page 193. Add your own ideas for solutions and results, and add ideas from the Listenings.
Group B: Complete the chart with your answers from page 195. Add your own ideas for solutions and results, and add ideas from the Listenings.

city: _____ topic: _____		
problem	**solution**	**result**

PREPARATION FOR SPEAKING

DESCRIBING A TOPIC

1 ▶ 8.5 Listen to Iman again. Then write the words and phrases from the box to complete the paragraph.

PRISM Online Workbook

> because   More and more   This is   This means   With all of

(1)_____ people are living in cities than in the countryside. (2)_____ that cities have a lot of traffic problems (3)_____ many people use their cars to go to work or school or to shop ... or whatever. (4)_____ these cars, it takes more time and gas to travel around the city. (5)_____ expensive for people, and the pollution is very bad in some places.

DESCRIBING A PROBLEM

2 ▶ 8.6 Write the verbs in the simple past. Then listen to Steve Miller and check your answers.

PRISM Online Workbook

Each passenger (1)_____ (wait) to buy a ticket, and then they (2)_____ (go) to the gate. At the gate, they (3)_____ (put) the ticket into the machine. Then the gate (4)_____ (open), and then they (5)_____ (take) their ticket from the machine. Now, this (6)_____ (take) a long time, and more people (7)_____ (start) to live and work in London, so we (8)_____ (need) a faster ticket system. And this (9)_____ (be) the Oyster card.

3 Which verbs are irregular past tense verbs?

PRONUNCIATION FOR SPEAKING

-d / -ed in regular simple past verbs

When a verb ends in these sounds, it is pronounced as /t/:	When a verb ends with a vowel sound or these consonant sounds, it is pronounced as /d/:	When a regular verb ends with a /t/ or /d/ sound, it is pronounced as /ɪd/:
sto**p** /p/	gra**b** /b/	visi**t** /t/
lau**gh** /f/	jo**g** /g/	deci**de** /d/
mi**ss** /s/	sa**ve** /v/	
li**ke** /k/	bu**zz** /z/	
fini**sh** /ʃ/	massa**ge** /ʒ/	
wa**tch** /tʃ/	chan**ge** /dʒ/	
	cli**mb** /m/	
	liste**n** /n/	
	trave**l** /l/	
	brea**the** /ð/	

4 ▶ 8.7 Listen and repeat the verbs in the past tense.

happened _____	needed _____	showed _____
changed _____	waited _____	watched _____
visited _____	asked _____	opened _____
guessed _____	helped _____	started _____

5 ▶ 8.7 Listen again. What sound do you hear at the end of each verb? Write /t/, /d/ or /ɪd/ next to each verb in Exercise 4.

DESCRIBING A SOLUTION

6 Put the words and phrases in order to make statements.

1 a subway / build / They / had to / .

_____

2 could / ride / People /bikes / for free / .

_____

3 The cities / carpooling / started / for workers / .

_____

4 There is / that moves / an inside /sidewalk / .

_____

5 is / faster / The Oyster card / .

_____

6 can tap / to pay / People / credit cards / .

_____

DESCRIBING RESULTS

7 Look at the problems, solutions, and results in the chart. Match the correct problems, solutions, and results. Then write them in the space provided.

problem	solution	result
There was no public transportation, so people had to drive everywhere.	One solution is self-driving cars.	So, these cars are safer because there are fewer accidents.
There are a lot of bad drivers, so there are a lot of accidents.	so Transport for London started Oyster cards.	That way, there were fewer cars, and workers felt better.
It took a long time because people waited to buy tickets and go through the gate,	One solution was carpooling.	The result is that it is very fast and easy.

1 _____

_____

2 _____

_____

3 _____

_____

8 Work with a partner. Take turns describing the results in Exercise 7. Use the phrases below to help you.

I think it was a good solution.

I don't think it was a good solution.

Why? Because …

That means …

SPEAKING TASK

Describe a transportation problem, solutions, and results.

PREPARE

1 Look back at the table in Critical Thinking. Review your notes and add any new information you want to include in your presentation.

2 Organize your talk by:

- introducing the topic.
- talking about the problem.
- talking about ideas for solutions.
- talking about what happened (the results).

3 Refer to the task checklist below as you prepare your talk.

TASK CHECKLIST	✔
Describe the topic.	
Describe the problem.	
Describe the solutions.	
Describe the results.	
Use *because* and *so* in the solutions and results.	
Use irregular simple past verbs correctly.	
Use correct pronunciation for regular simple past verbs with /t/, /d/, and /ɪd/.	

PRESENT

4 Work with a partner from your group. Take turns practicing your talk. Use your notes and the photos of the city to help you.

5 Work with a partner from the other group. Take turns describing the solution to the transportation problem in Los Angeles or Mexico City.

DISCUSS

6 Discuss the questions in class.

1 Which city had the best solution?
2 Is that solution a good idea for your city / country? Why or why not?

ON CAMPUS

FINDING HELP

PREPARING TO LISTEN

1 Work with a partner. Discuss the questions

    1 What kinds of problems do students have in college?

    2 What can students do when they have problems?

STUDENT SUCCESS CENTER	Home	Advice	Search	🔍

Do you feel overwhelmed by the stress of all the things you have to do: schoolwork, part-time job, and family life? Are you having problems in your relationships with friends, roommates, or family?

The STUDENT SUCCESS CENTER can help you with your problems!

- Private, one-on-one counseling with a psychologist
- Workshops on time management
- No appointments necessary—walk in any time
- Open 24 hours a day, 7 days a week

---

2 Read the information about the Student Success Center. Then choose a word from the box that best matches the definition.

success   counseling   overwhelmed   relationships

    1 having too much to do: _____

    2 connections with other people: _____

    3 advice and help for problems: _____

    4 a good result _____

WHILE LISTENING

3 ▶ 8.8 Listen to the interview and choose the correct answer.

    1 What is the job of Ken Davidson?

       a psychologist   **b** student

    2 What does he talk about?

       a the work of the Student Success Center

       b students' relationships with their classmates

4 ▶ 8.8 Listen again and write *T* (true) or *F* (false).

_____ 1 Ken Davidson is a director.

_____ 2 The Student Success Center helps students who need medical care.

_____ 3 Many students are overwhelmed because they have to find time to work and study.

_____ 4 A counselor usually talks to students about their problems and gives advice.

_____ 5 Professor Davidson believes that students should ask for help when they need it.

SKILLS

Finding help

Many students feel stress, depression, or loneliness in college. If you have problems, ask for help. Talk to a friend, a teacher, or a counselor.

REAL-WORLD APPLICATION

5 Work in a small group. Read the problems below. Then think of some advice that you could give for each problem.

1 I feel overwhelmed. I have too much to do!
2 My classes are really difficult!
3 I don't get along with my roommate.
4 I'm worried about finding a job after college.
5 I'm homesick. I miss my family and my friends.

6 Work in groups of three students. Choose one of the problems below. Add extra details. Make some notes and prepare to explain your problem.

A I was so excited to come to college, but I'm very lonely here. It's difficult for me to make friends, and I miss my family and friends back home. How can I make some friends?

B I work during the day, and I take classes in the evenings. My boss just offered me a better job with more money, but it means I'll be very busy. I'm worried that I won't have enough time to study. Should I take the job?

C I'm in my second year of college, studying business and finance. I want to change my major, because I'm more interested in science. But my father wants me to study business so that I can help him in the family business after I graduate. Should I change my major?

7 Using your notes, explain your problem to the group. In your group, discuss different solutions for each problem and decide on the best one.

PAIRWORK ACTIVITIES

STUDENT A

UNIT 1
DISCUSSION, EXERCISE 8

Think about what you heard in Listening 1 and Listening 2. Ask Student B these questions about the person in photo D on page 25.

What's her name?
Where's she from?
Why is she famous?
Who are her parents?

Read this information. Then answer Student B's questions about the person in photo C on page 25.

Name: Larry Page
Country: the United States
Job: engineer, computer scientist, businessman
Famous: started Google with a friend
Parents: father, Carl Page, computer scientist / mother, Gloria Page, computer scientist

UNIT 1
PREPARATION FOR SPEAKING, EXERCISE 1

Spell the words for your partner.

1 M–E–X–I–C–A–N
2 S–O–U–T–H – K–O–R–E–A–N
3 E–G–Y–P–T–I–A–N
4 E–M–I–R–A–T–I

UNIT 2
ON CAMPUS, EXERCISE 5

Student Name: _____
Student ID #: Y23672280
Academic Advisor: Prof. Gerald Manning
Office #: 43
Advising meeting: Monday, September 5, 11 am
Dormitory: Douglas Hall
Resident Advisor: Susan Lam

UNIT 4
DISCUSS, EXERCISE 5

The University of Alpha

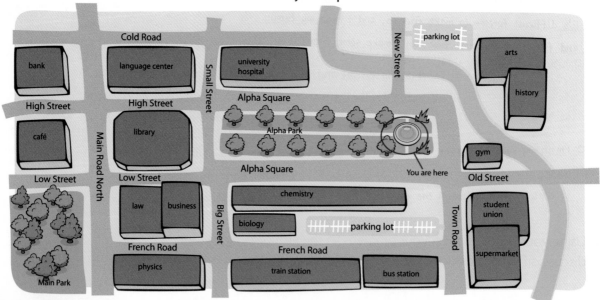

UNIT 4
SPEAKING TASK, EXERCISE 3
Group A (Student A)

1 Work with other students from Group A and practice giving directions from the fountain to places 1–5 on the map of The University of Alpha. Take notes.

1 the bank
2 the language center
3 the physics building
4 the history building
5 the supermarket

UNIT 5
LISTENING 2, EXERCISE 4

About you

My name's Alan Green, and I'm from Portland, Oregon, in the U.S. I'm a student here at the University of Yukon. I would like to work at the sports center after I graduate.

I'm strong, in great shape, and I love sports. I can speak English and French. My favorite sports are soccer and basketball. I can also teach karate and judo.

UNIT 8
CRITICAL THINKING, EXERCISE 2
Group A

1 What is the topic?
2 What was the problem?
3 What was the solution?
4 Was it a good solution? (What was the result?)

Topic:
Traffic problems and solutions for Mexico City, Santa Fe District

Mexico City is one of the biggest cities in the world. There are 850,000 car trips each day there. Forty-one percent of the car trips are for business reasons. Pollution is also a problem. Forty-nine percent of the pollution comes from cars. There are no subways, trains, or buses, so people have to drive everywhere. And businesses need to have parking lots, so it costs them more money. The traffic is bad for workers, too. It takes too much time to drive to work, so they feel tired at work. They spend more time driving to work and more money for gas than people in cities with good public transportation. One solution is sharing transportation with others. For example, workers use carpooling or bike-sharing. This way, there are fewer cars and workers feel better.

STUDENT B
UNIT 1
DISCUSSION, EXERCISE 8

Read this information. Then answer Student A's questions about the person in photo D on page 25.

> **Name:** Ursula Burns
> **Country:** the United States
> **Job:** businesswoman
> **Famous:** first African-American female CEO of large company in the U.S.
> **Parent:** mother—Olga Burns, child-care center owner

Think about what you heard in Listening 1 and Listening 2. Ask Student A these questions about the person in photo C on page 25.

What's his name?
Where's he from?
Why is he famous?
Who are his parents?

PREPARATION FOR SPEAKING, EXERCISE 1

Spell the words for your partner.

5 J–A–P–A–N–E–S–E
6 T–U–R–K–I–S–H
7 B–R–A–Z–I–L–I–A–N
8 C–O–L–O–M–B–I–A–N

UNIT 2
ON CAMPUS, EXERCISE 5

Student Name:	_____
Student ID #:	Y23900649
Academic Advisor:	Prof. Robert Mendez
Office #:	360
Advising meeting:	Thursday, September 8, 9 am
Dormitory:	Fenwick Hall
Resident Advisor:	Thomas Li

UNIT 4
DISCUSS, EXERCISE 4

The University of Beta

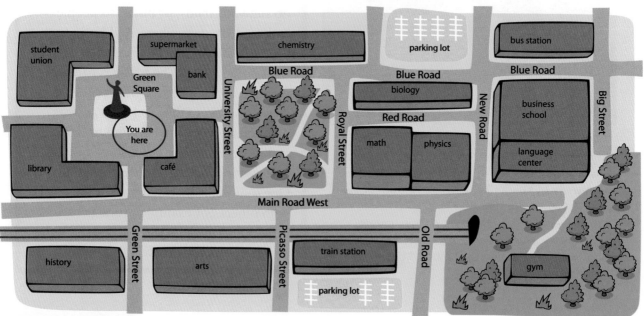

UNIT 4
SPEAKING TASK, EXERCISE 3
Group B (Student B)

1 Work with other students from Group B and practice giving directions from the statue to places 1–5 on the map of The University of Beta. Take notes.

1 the history building
2 the train station
3 the physics building
4 the bus station
5 the gym

UNIT 5
LISTENING 2, EXERCISE 4

About you

I'm Lucy Lau, and I'm from Vancouver, Canada. I speak English, French, and Cantonese. I have a degree in sports science. In Vancouver, I teach zumba, pilates, and yoga. I'm also a good tennis player. I think it is important to be a kind and polite. A fitness instructor should help people. I would like to work with you

UNIT 8
CRITICAL THINKING, EXERCISE 2
Group B
1 What is the topic?
2 What was the problem?
3 What was the solution?
4 Was it a good solution?
  (What was the result?)

Solution to traffic problems in Los Angeles, California, U.S.

Los Angeles is a big city with a lot of people and big traffic problems. People spend 72 hours or more sitting in traffic every year. All of this sitting is not good for people's health. The pollution is bad in Los Angeles because there are so many cars on the road. There is public transportation, but most people still like to drive because it is a car culture. One new solution is something called a self-driving car. It drives itself, so you don't have to drive it. You can just sit and enjoy the ride. These cars are safer because not everyone is a good driver! So, self-driving cars can stop accidents from happening. Workers can relax more and worry less when they drive, so it's good for their health and work.

GLOSSARY OF KEY VOCABULARY

Words that are part of the Academic Word List are noted with an **A** in this glossary.

UNIT 1 PEOPLE

LISTENING 1

brother (n) a boy or man who has the same parents as you

doctor (n) a person whose job is to help sick or hurt people

engineer (n) someone whose job is to design, build, or repair machines, engines, roads, bridges, etc.

family (n) a group of people who are related to each other, especially parents and children

father (n) someone's male parent (a man)

manager (n) someone in control of an office, store, team, etc.

mother (n) someone's female parent (a woman)

sister (n) a girl or woman who has the same parents as you

student (n) someone who is studying at a school or college

LISTENING 2

businessman (n) a man who works in business, usually having an important job

businesswoman (n) a woman who works in business, usually having an important job

chef (n) the main person who cooks food at a restaurant or hotel

scientist (n) someone who studies science or works in science

teacher (n) someone whose job is to teach in a school, college, etc.

writer (n) someone whose job is to write books, stories, articles, etc.

UNIT 2 CLIMATE

LISTENING 1

cold (adj) having a low temperature

fall (n) the season of the year between summer and winter

hot (adj) having a high temperature

snow (n) soft, white pieces of frozen water that fall from the sky

spring (n) the season of the year between winter and summer

temperature (n) how hot or cold something is

weather (n) the temperature or conditions outside; for example, hot, cold, sunny, snowy, etc.

LISTENING 2

desert (n) a large, hot, dry area with very few plants, like the Sahara Desert

forest (n) a large area of trees growing closely together

island (n) an area of land that has water around it

mountain (n) a very high hill

park (n) a large area of grass and trees, usually very beautiful, and everybody can use it

sea (n) a large area of salt water

sky (n) the area above the Earth where you can see clouds and the sun

UNIT 3 LIFESTYLE

LISTENING 1

do homework (v phr) to do the work teachers give students to do at home

exercise (v) to do physical activity to make your body strong and healthy

go online (v phr) to use the Internet

play computer games (v phr) to use a game that is played on a computer

sleep (v) to rest with your eyes closed and your mind unconscious

text (v) to use a cell phone to write and send a short message

watch TV (v phr) to look at the television for a period of time

LISTENING 2

busy (adj) if you are busy, you are working hard and doing many things

café (n) a small restaurant for tea, coffee, and snacks

go out (v) to spend time with friends outside your home

gym (n) a place where you can go to exercise and keep fit

parent (n) your mother or father

study (v) to learn a particular subject in school or college, or by reading books

UNIT 4 PLACES

LISTENING 1

building (n) a house, school, hospital, or office with walls and a roof

directions (n) information that tells you how to get to a place

library (n) a place where people can come to study with a lot of books for people to take home

location Ⓐ (n) the place where something is

map (n) a picture that shows where countries, towns, roads, and rivers, etc. are

safe (adj) not dangerous

LISTENING 2

campus (n) a large area for university buildings

department store (n) a store where you can buy many different things, such as clothes, furniture, toys, etc.

food court (n) a place with many small restaurants, usually in a shopping mall

hospital (n) a place to get help if you are sick or hurt

movie theater (n) a place where people go to watch movies

parking lot (n) an area outside an office, mall, etc. for cars

playground (n) a place with special equipment for children to play on

restroom (n) a room in a public building where there are toilets

shopping mall (n) a large building with many different kinds of stores inside

supermarket (n) a large store where you can buy food

UNIT 5 JOBS

LISTENING 1

advice (n) suggestions about what you think someone should do

boring (adj) not interesting or exciting

earn (v) to get money for doing work

hard (adj) difficult to do or understand

help (v) to make it easier for someone to do something

job Ⓐ (n) the work a person does to get money

work (v) to do a job, especially a job you do to get money

LISTENING 2

example (n) something that is typical of what you are talking about

in shape (p phr) healthy and strong, especially from exercising

kind (adj) wanting to help others and show you care about them

polite (adj) behaving in a way that shows good manners and respect for others

strong (adj) physically powerful; not weak

teach (v) to give lessons at a school or university

UNIT 6 HOMES AND BUILDINGS

LISTENING 1

ceiling (n) the top of a room that you can see when you look up

floor (n) what you walk on inside a building

furniture (n) things such as chairs, tables, and beds that you put in a home or office

room (n) what the inside of a building is made up of

wall (n) one of the sides of a room

wood (n) the hard material that trees are made of

LISTENING 2

cheap (adj) not costing a lot of money

expensive (adj) costing a lot of money

far (adv) not near or close in location

modern (adj) using the newest ideas, design, technology, etc.

near (adv) very close in location; not far

noisy (adj) making a lot of noise

quiet (adj) making little noise or no noise

UNIT 7 FOOD AND CULTURE

LISTENING 1

dish (n) food prepared in a special way and given a name

fast food (n) food that is served very quickly in a restaurant because it is already prepared, like hamburgers and French fries

fish (n) an animal that lives in water and swims using its tail and fins

international (adj) relating to two or more countries

meat (n) the parts of animals that we eat

rice (n) small, white or brown grains from a plant that are cooked and eaten

vegetables (n) plants that we eat

LISTENING 2

culture Ⓐ (n) the usual way of living in a country or for a group of people

enjoy (v) to get pleasure from something

favorite (adj) your favorite person or thing is the one you like the best

healthy (adj) good for your health

home-cooked (adj) food cooked at home

meal (n) the food that you eat at breakfast, lunch, or dinner

UNIT 8 TRANSPORTATION

LISTENING 1

bus (n) a big type of car that takes many people around a city

passenger (n) someone who travels in a car, bus, etc., but doesn't drive it

subway (n) train that travels underground, usually in a city

taxi (n) a car with a driver who you pay to take you somewhere

ticket (n) a small piece of paper that shows you paid to do something

train (n) a long, thin type of car that travels on metal tracks and carries people or things

travel (v) to go from one place to another, usually over a long distance

trip (n) a time when you go to a place for a short time and come back again

LISTENING 2

accident (n) a situation that is not planned and that causes pain or problems

bike (n) a type of transportation with two wheels that you sit on and move by turning two pedals (= parts you press with your feet)

gas (n) what cars need in order to drive

idea (n) a suggestion or plan for doing something

problem (n) something that makes life difficult and needs a solution

sidewalk (n) a hard path for people to walk on next to a road

traffic (n) the cars, trucks, etc. driving on the road

VIDEO AND AUDIO SCRIPTS

UNIT 1

▶ **The Life of a Businesswoman**

Narrator: Karen has a very busy job. She's a financial trader in an office. She helps people make money.

Karen lives with her family in New York City. She has a beautiful apartment there.

But her life is busy at home, too—with a husband, four children, and a dog. So, she has a person to walk the dog, a person to clean the house, and a person to make schedules for her children.

Karen: So, this is the motherboard. Each child has a different color coding. It's a bit of a complicated life.

Narrator: Everyone is very busy.

Karen loves her apartment. Her favorite room is the living room, where she can relax and read after work. She loves to look at the city through her windows.

But she and her husband also love their house in the country. This is Scott. He's a financial trader, and his life is very busy, too.

For Scott, it's important to exercise every day. In his free time, he likes to ride his bike and do triathlons.

🔊 **1.1**

1 introduce
2 please
3 Peru
4 Turkey
5 twenty
6 eighteen
7 study
8 business
9 computer
10 college

🔊 **1.2**

Carlos: Hi, hello. I'm Carlos. I'm going to tell you about Koko. She's a **student** in our class. She's 18, and she's from Japan. Her **family's** from Sapporo. Her father's a teacher. She wants to study English in college.

Kerry: A-l-l right! Thank you, Carlos. So, Koko. It's your turn. Please introduce the student next to you.

Koko: Hello! Yes! I'm going to tell you about Hussain. This is Hussain. He's from Al Ain. Al Ain is in, the uh …

Kerry: Un-*it*-ed … *A*-rab … *Em*-ir-ates.

Koko: Yes … the UAE! Hussain's from Al Ain. It's in the UAE. He's 20. His family's from Al Ain. He has two younger **sisters** and one younger **brother**. He likes soccer, and his favorite player is Lionel Messi. Hussain wants to study business in college.

Kerry: Thank you, Koko. Great job. So, Hussain. Please introduce the student next to you.

Hussain: Hi! I'm going to tell you about Nehir. Nehir is 19. She's from Turkey. She has a brother. Her family has a hotel. Her **mother** and **father** are the **managers**. Nehir wants to study business in college.

Kerry: Thank you, Hussain. Nehir—your turn!

Nehir: Hello. I'm going to tell you about Carlos. He's 19. He's from Peru. His father's an **engineer**, and his mother's a **doctor**. Carlos wants to study computer science in college.

Kerry: Thank you, Nehir.

🔊 **1.3**

A

Kerry: Who's your best friend, Yasemin?

Yasemin: Her name is Meral.

Kerry: How old is she?

Yasemin: She's 20.

Kerry: Is she from Turkey?

Mehmet: Yes, but she isn't from Ankara like me. She's from Izmir.

B

Ryo: Excuse me, Kerry. Are you from Toronto?

Kerry: No, no, I'm not from Canada. I'm from the United States. But my grandparents are Canadian. They're not from Toronto. They're from Montreal.

Ryo: Are your parents American?

Kerry: Yes—and my sisters. We're all American.

🔊 **1.4**

1 writer	4 businesswoman
2 teacher	5 chef
3 businessman	6 scientist

🔊 **1.5**

Marie: Hi, everybody! Good morning! My name is Marie.

All: Hi. / Morning. / Hello.

Marie: OK, so I'm going to tell you about a famous person. She's from the United States. It's photo "a." Who is this, in the photo?

Student: Um, is she a **writer**?

Marie: Yes! That's it! She's a writer. Her name's Alice Waters. She writes a lot about food. She's also a **chef** and restaurant owner—a real **businesswoman**. She's famous for her work with healthy food. She's from California. Her family's American. Her husband's name is Steven. He's a **businessman**. He sells healthy food. She also has a daughter. Her daughter's also a writer and a chef. Her family's very creative! Food's the family business.

Clare: Thanks, Marie. Hi, everyone! My name is Clare. Now, I'm going to tell you about my person. Do you know him? In photo "b"? He's Salman Khan. He's also American. Salman's a **scientist** and a **teacher**. He's famous for his free school, the Khan Academy. All the classes are on the Internet. The students are from many countries. Salman's from California, but his father's from Bangladesh, and his mother's from India. His wife's a doctor, and they have a son and a daughter.

🔊 **1.6**

1 I'm going to tell you about a famous person from Mexico.

2 Ana García is a famous Mexican chef.

3 This is Haruki Murakami.

4 He's a famous Japanese writer.

🔊 **1.7**

1 Karim Abdel Aziz is a famous actor.

2 Karim's father is Mohammed Abdel Aziz.

3 He's a film director.

4 Karim's aunt is Samira Muhsin.

5 She's an actor.

🔊 **1.8**

Conversation A

Carlos: Excuse me, Professor Baker?

Professor: Yes, how can I help you?

Carlos: My name is Carlos Mendoza. I'm a new student.

Professor: Oh, yes, I remember. You sent me an email.

Carlos: Yes. I'm sorry I'm late.

Professor: That's OK. Welcome to the class.

Carlos: Thank you. Is it possible to have some information about the class?

Professor: Yes, of course. Here's a copy of the syllabus. Why don't you take a look at it and ask me next class if you have any questions.

Carlos: OK. Thank you.

Professor: And make sure you get on the class website.

Carlos: I will.

Professor: All right. I'll see you in class on Thursday.

Carlos: Thank you very much, professor.

Conversation B

Tony: Hi, how are you doing?

Lisa: Fine, thanks … . Hey … can I borrow a pen?

Tony: Sure. Here you go.

Lisa: Thanks a lot. I'm Lisa.

Tony: I'm Tony.

Lisa: Hi, Tony. Nice to meet you.

Tony: Yeah, you too. Is this your first semester?

Lisa: Yeah. How about you?

Tony: Yeah. Me, too.

Lisa: Where are you from?

Tony: France.

Lisa: Really? Wow. Your English is really good.

Tony: Thanks.

Lisa: What part of France are you from?

Tony: I'm from Paris. Have you been there?

Lisa: No, but I'd love to go some time.

Tony: Hey, do you want to get a coffee after class?

Lisa: Sure. That sounds great.

UNIT 2

▶ **How Deserts are Formed**

This is the Sonoran Desert in North America. It's 2,000 miles north of the equator.

In the summer, the temperature can reach 122 degrees Fahrenheit. But it's not a desert because it's hot. It's a desert because there isn't much water.

Here it only rains about three inches a year, so there are very different plants and animals in a desert than in a rainforest. Where does the hot, dry air come from? It comes from near the equator.

Because the Earth spins, hot air from the equator moves high in the air, travels north, and then comes down in the Sonoran Desert. And this doesn't just happen in North America. It happens around the world.

There's the Thar Desert in India, the Arabian Desert in the Middle East, and, of course, the Sahara Desert in North Africa. Hot dry air from near the equator made all of these deserts. That's why all of these places have hot, dry climates.

◀)) **2.1**

1 Take a look at the photos.

2 They are all from one place.

3 There's a beautiful beach next to a big lake.

4 It's winter, and there's a mountain.

5 It's hot, and there's sand.

◀)) **2.2**

Professor: OK, so today I want to talk about a place with extreme **temperatures**. Take a look at the photos. What seasons do you see?

Student 1: Summer

Professor: Uh, huh.

Student 2: Winter

Professor: Yes, that's right.

Student 3: **Fall**

Professor: And?

Student 4: **Spring**?

Professor: Yes, and they're all from one place—Minnesota—in the United States. It's in the middle of the country next to Canada. So, there's **cold** air from the north and warm air from the south. This can create extreme temperatures.

Let's look at photo "a". What can we see? Well, it's a **hot** day in summer. And, there's a beautiful lake and a beach. There's a blue sky, and it's sunny. There are 10,000 lakes in Minnesota, so people like to swim and fish.

Now here, in photo "b", it's winter. There's lots of **snow** and a forest. It's also very cold. The temperature can get to minus 30 degrees F.

In photo "c", you can see it's fall. The temperature is a little cold, and the trees change color to red and orange. There are many forests in Minnesota, so it's very beautiful.

And now we see spring in photo "d". After the cold **weather**, spring is welcome in Minnesota. The weather is warm and it rains, so the flowers grow.

As you can see, Minnesota is a place with four seasons and extreme temperatures in winter. But, it's a beautiful place, so people like to do things outside.

🔊 2.3

1 Canada gets a lot of snow in winter.
2 Summer in Washington, D.C. begins in June. It gets very hot.
3 Spring in New York is from March to May. There are a lot of beautiful flowers.
4 In fall, the trees change color from green to orange or red.
5 In Korea, Japan, and China, the rainy season begins in June and ends in July. It gets very wet.
6 The dry season in Brazil begins in May. There is not a lot of rain.

🔊 2.4

1 There's a river in the photo.
2 There's water in the lake.
3 There are stones on the beach.
4 There's a small town in the mountains.
5 There are black clouds in the sky.
6 There are extreme temperatures in the winter.

🔊 2.5

Daniela: OK, so, good morning, everybody. I'm Daniela. OK, so, uh, I'm going to talk about two photos of a place in spring. I'm from Naples in Italy, and I don't like to talk about cold places or places in winter—no, really, it's true!

OK, so here's my first photo. This isn't in Italy. It's in Turkey. It's actually an **island**. And there's a small town here. You can see there is a white building. It's a beautiful day in spring—blue **sky**, very sunny, very nice. There's a nice **forest**, and it's good to go there when it's a

hot day. And there's the **sea**, which is beautiful and blue.

So I chose this photo because ...

Altan: Hello, everybody! OK, so, I'm Altan. I'm from Samsun. Uh, Samsun is in Turkey, I'm Turkish, and Samsun's a city by the Black Sea. But, OK, so today I'm going to talk about a different place.

Here's my first photo. It's a beautiful place. You can see there's a big **mountain**, and there are trees here. It's sunny, but it's a cold day in autumn. Can you see the color of the trees? All red and yellow.

So, where is this beautiful place? Well, it's in South Korea. This is Seoraksan National **Park**. It's a famous park. A lot of people go there. Here's another photo of the park ...

🔊 2.6

a Good morning, everybody.
b I'm going to talk about two photos of a place in spring.
c OK, so here's my first photo.
d Hello, everybody! I'm Altan.
e I'm from Samsun. Uh, Samsun is in Turkey.
f Here's my first photo.
g Here's another photo of the park.

🔊 2.7

Khaled: Hello, everybody! OK, so I'm Khaled. I'm from Port Said in Egypt. Today I'm going to talk about two photos of a place in spring. Here's my first photo. You can see there's a big mountain. There's a lot of snow. And there are trees. The trees are orange and red. Right, so where is this place? It's in Japan. This is Mount Fuji.

Here's another photo of the mountain. There's a path, and you can see there are people there. There are a lot of white clouds below. It's a beautiful place. I want to go there.

Maya: Hi, welcome to campus. I'm Maya. What's your name?

Lee: Lixin Chen. Lixin is my first name.

Maya: How do you spell that?

Lee: L-I-X-I-N. Li-shin. But you can call me Lee.

Maya: OK! Nice to meet you! Where are you from?

Lee: I'm from China.

Maya: And you're a freshman, right?

Lee: A ... what? Can you say that again?

Maya: You're a freshman. This is your first year here at college.

Lee: Oh ... Yes. This is my first year. What about you?

Maya: I'm a senior. I'm graduating next June.

Lee: Wow ... that's great!

Maya: So ... do you have any questions?

Lee: Oh ... yes ... em ... I have a meeting tomorrow with Professor ... em ... Peter Baker. Do you know who he is?

Maya: Oh, he's probably your advisor. He's going to help you choose your classes. What's his office number?

Lee: Er ... let me see. Williams 521.

Maya: That's in the Science Building. It's not far.

Lee: OK, thanks.

Maya: Are you living in a dorm?

Lee: Yes. My roommate is really nice. She's from Brazil.

Maya: That's good.

Lee: Oh yes, ... I do have another question. If I have a problem in the dorm, who do I speak to?

Maya: Yes. That's the RA.

Lee: The RA? I'm sorry, I don't understand.

Maya: RA means resident advisor. We say "RA" for short. If you have problems, you should speak to him ... or her.

Lee: OK. What is the word again?

Maya: Resident advisor. You can just say RA.

Lee: RA. OK. Thank you!

UNIT 3

▶ The Age Wave

More than 50,000 people now live in a place called The Villages in Florida. Everyone is at least 55 years old. The Villages looks and feels like a real town, but it isn't.

Most of them don't work anymore. They spend their days playing golf, working in their yards, and riding bicycles. The Villages even has its own cable television station and news team. The people there may be older, but they are happy and active.

This kind of place is quite new in history. Americans now live longer than ever before. After they finish working, many Americans now live for 30 or more years.

Where do they live and what kind of lifestyles do they have? Here at The Villages the focus is on staying active. The people here work out in the gym—they lift weights, walk on treadmills, and ride stationary bikes.

They even rollerblade through the streets. But will their children and grandchildren have the same lifestyle when they are older?

🔊 3.1

Speaker A: What's your name?

Jennifer: My name is Jennifer.

Speaker A: Are you from New York?

Jennifer: No. I'm from Toronto.

🔊 3.2

1 What do you want to watch on TV?

2 How many hours do you sleep every night?

3 Who's between the ages of 13 and 19?

4 Do you play computer games?

5 It's important for people to exercise.

6 Do you text a lot?

🔊 3.3

Professor: Good morning, everybody.

Students: Good morning. / Hello. / Hi.

Professor: So, today we're going to look at lifestyles ... the lifestyles of teenagers. So, who's between the ages of 13 and 19?

Students: I am. I'm 19. / Me, too. / I'm 18.

Professor: Then, you are all teenagers. Anyone else? OK, so let's talk about **sleep**. How many hours do you sleep every night? Yes, Jose?

Jose: Um ... I sleep maybe six or seven hours every night.

Professor: OK. Anyone else? Yes, Beatrice, how many hours do you sleep?

Beatrice: I don't sleep a lot. I sleep maybe five hours.

Professor: OK. Yes, Ana, and you?

Ana: Not enough. I only sleep five or six hours a night during the week.

Professor: You're right. That's not enough, especially for teens. How many hours do you think teens need?

Jose: A lot!

Professor: Yes, you're right about that. Teens need ten or more hours every night. So, what do you usually do at night? Are you busy? Yes, Jose?

Jose: At night, I like to **play computer games**.

Professor: OK. Anyone else? Yes, Maria.

Maria: Well, I usually **watch TV**.

Beatrice: I **go online** or **text** friends.

Professor: And then you **do** the **homework** for this class, of course.
So, let me ask you, what do you do on Saturday and Sunday? Yes, Sung-oh?

Sung-oh: Well, I also play computer games on Saturday and Sunday.

Professor: Uh-huh, and what about you, Jiang?

Jiang: Um, well, I watch TV or go online.

Professor: What else do you do? Do you **exercise**? Exercise is also very important for teens. It's important for all of us. Do you exercise, Eunji?

Eunji: Uh, to be honest, I don't really exercise.

Professor: Anyone else? ... Well, let's think of some things teens need to do to stay healthy and do well in school ...

🔊 **3.4**

1

A: Excuse me. I'd like to ask you a question.

B: Don't talk to me. Not now.

2

A: Can I have a few minutes of your time?

B: Sure. No problem.

3

A: Pardon me. Do you have a minute?

B: No. Sorry, I don't.

🔊 **3.5**

April: Good morning! Can I ask you ... ?

Woman 1: Sorry, sorry! No time! No time!

April: Excuse me! Do you have ... ?

Woman 2: Sorry! Can't stop! That's my bus!

April: Excuse me! Can I have a few minutes of your time?

Jasvinder: Uh, yes, sure.

April: Great! My name's April. I'm a college student, and I'm asking people questions about their lifestyle. I'd like to ask you some questions—is that OK?

Jasvinder: Yes, no problem. I'm Jasvinder.

April: Great! Nice to meet you, Jasvinder! OK, so, uh, well, I'll just start, then? OK, so do you live with your **parents**?

Jasvinder: Yes.

April: And do you work or **study**?

Jasvinder: Oh, I study—I'm a student.

April: And what do you study?

Jasvinder: I study biology. I'd like to be a scientist.

April: Hmm. OK, and do you have a **busy** lifestyle?

Jasvinder: Yes, I think so. I have a lot of homework.

April: I see, OK, and what things do you do to relax?

Jasvinder: Hm. Well, I go to a **gym**. I exercise a lot.

April: Really?

Jasvinder: Yes. I am happy when I exercise.

April: Yes, I know what you mean. And when do you go to the gym?

Jasvinder: Oh, every day.

April: Every day? Wow. OK, and what other things do you do? Do you go to the movies for example?

Jasvinder: No, not really. I watch movies on my computer at home.

April: I see. And what about your friends? When do you **go out** with them?

Jasvinder: Oh, well, I have some friends at the gym. But I also go out on Saturday afternoons. We go to a **café** and have some coffee and talk about ... well, we talk about life, people we know, that kind of thing.

April: I think I know what you mean! OK, so ...

🔊 **3.6**

This is Claudia. She's from Canada. She takes the bus to the university every day. The bus comes at 7:30. Claudia arrives at 8:30. She has a biology class at nine on Tuesday and Thursday. On Wednesday, she has lunch with her friends at 12:30. On Thursday, Claudia has an English class at three o'clock in the afternoon. She goes to the movies with her family on Friday evening. On Saturday, she exercises in the morning. On Sunday, she does her homework in the evening. She has a busy week.

🔊 **3.7**

texts	studies
sleeps	watches
needs	chooses
goes	

🔊 **3.8**

1 gets
2 wears
3 misses
4 has
5 teaches
6 takes
7 plays
8 laughs

🔊 **3.9**

Joe: I live on campus, and I usually study in my dorm room. But sometimes it's difficult to study because I have two roommates. We often just talk or play computer games. So ... I go to bed late ... like, two or three in the morning. My first class starts at 10:30, so I can sleep late. I like that. I'm not a morning person!

Fabiola: I never have enough time to study. I'm a part-time student and I work on Tuesday and Thursday from two until ten in the evening. So I have all my classes on Monday, Wednesday, and Friday. On those days, I start at eight in the morning and I finish at 7:30 in the evening, and then I just go to bed! The best time for me to study is on Tuesday and Thursday mornings, before work, but sometimes I have to help my family on those days.

Michaela: I'm on the college basketball team, so I have to organize my time well. I have practice every morning at seven, and most days I have classes after that. I study during the afternoons and in the evenings ... after dinner. I usually go to the library until about nine or ten. On the weekends, we often have games, so I can't study then.

UNIT 4

▶ **Urbanization in China**

Today, more and more people live in cities. In 1970, only two cities in the world had more than 10 million people.

Now, there are more than 20, and the number is growing. These urban areas are important for our future. And there's a lot of work to keep a megacity going and growing.

Welcome to Shanghai, one of China's largest cities. Its skyline—the view of its buildings against the sky—has changed a lot over the past 20 years.

One man has an interesting record of the changes in his hometown. Two times every year, Yao Jin Yang goes to the top of the Oriental Pearl Tower, and he takes pictures of the Shanghai skyline.

Mr. Yao started taking pictures in 1993. Then, this tower was the tallest building in Shanghai and had the best view of the city. Today the city looks very different. His photos show how fast people can change their world.

In China, lots of people started moving from the country to the city more than 30 years ago. Now, 10,000 people move to Shanghai every week.

This kind of change is happening all over China and in many parts of the world.

🔊 4.1

1 Where is this photo from?

2 ... there's a store here and a library there.

3 Yes, that's a bank over there.

4 The library is here.

🔊 4.2

Salesperson: Welcome, everyone. Thank you for coming to our presentation for our new app, familynet.

Families are very busy today. Every day parents go to work, and, well, children need to go everywhere. They go to school. They go to the park. They play sports or go to a friend's house. Often, teens can go places by themselves. But parents want to be sure they are **safe**. With the familynet app, they are. Parents can find the **location** of their children anywhere, anytime. And children can find the location of their parents anywhere, anytime. Do you know where your children are right now? Do you know which street or **building**? Do you have **directions** to find them? I do with this app. And, I have two teens and an eight year old.

Let me show you how it works.

Look at the screenshot, please. There's a **map**. You can see the location of three children. This is the location of my three children right now. This is my son. He's at the park. That's my daughter. She's between school and the **library**. And there's her little sister. She's next to the bus. The app will tell me when she gets home. That's nice, so I can meet her. My children are safe. I can see their location. For my teens, they can go places without their mom and dad. This makes them happy. And it makes their parents happy. You may think your teens will not like the app. My teens are no different. But, now they can go places when we can't take them. So, they like the app now. Our app is easy to use. Just download it to your phone and open it! Try it now to find everyone in your family.

🔊 4.3

1

A: Where's the library? Is it near here?

B: Yes, it's behind the river.

2

A: Is there a bank near here?

B: Yes. There's one over the bridge. Can you see it?

3

A: Where's the famous monument?

B: It's between the university and the river.

4

A: Excuse me. Where's the factory?

B: It's by the river.

5

A: I can't find the museum. Is it near here?

B: No. It's there on the left. It's next to the park.

6

A: Where's the university?

B: It's across from those houses.

7

A: Where can I find the train station?

B: It's in front of a tall building.

8

A: I'm looking for the fountain. Is it in the park?

B: Yes. It's there in the park.

🔊 **4.4**

Professor: OK, class. You now know your way around **campus**, but I know some of you like to go shopping. And it's very easy to get lost in a big **shopping mall**. So, today, let's practice what to say if you are lost. Everybody, look at the map, please. I'll begin. Ana, can you tell me where **parking lot** 1 is?

Ana: Yes, it's on West Street, across from entrance 1.

Professor: Good, Ana. Pedro, I'm at the **department store**. How do I get to the **movie theater**?

Pedro: Go out of the store and take a left on path A. When you get to path B, turn left again. The movie theater is on your right.

Professor: All right, Pedro! Hongmi, I'm on North Street. Can you tell me how to get to the **supermarket**?

Hongmi: Yes, go east. Then, take a right on East Street and follow it until you see the supermarket. It's on your right, next to the bus station.

Professor: Excellent, Hongmi! OK, now I'm lost. I'm in this shoe store. Excuse me, miss. Where is the **restroom**?

Luisa: Oh, that's easy. It's across from you next to the stairs.

Professor: Nice job, Luisa. OK, Jisoo. I'm at the movie theater. Can you tell me how to find the **playground**?

Jisoo: Um … yes. Go along path B and go through the **food court**. It's behind the food court and the shoe store.

Professor: OK, Jisoo! Now, I'm looking for the computer store. I'm at the food court. Where can I find it?

Ana: Just go south on path A. It's on your right between the department store and the elevators.

Professor: Very good, Ana. Thank you. Now, everyone, work with a partner and practice asking for and giving directions for the next map which is a **hospital**, I don't want you to get lost!

🔊 **4.5**

1 It's across from the business school.

2 It's in Green Square.

3 Go through Alpha Park to the student center.

4 It's in front of that big fountain. There—on the right.

5 OK, then, so we're at the language school.

6 Go along French Road.

7 There's one next to the train station.

8 It's there on the left. It's behind that school.

🔊 **4.6**

1 Where's the supermarket?

2 Is the physics building near here?

3 How do I get to the language center?

4 Can you tell me how to get to the history building?

5 I'm looking for the math building. Is it near here?

math building; physics building;
language center; student center

a Excuse me! Can you tell me how to get to
the history building, please?

b Excuse me! I think I'm lost. Is the physics
building near here?

c Excuse me! How do I get to the
language center?

1 Excuse me! Where's the student center,
please?

2 Excuse me! I think I'm lost. How do I get to
the chemistry building?

3 Excuse me! Can you tell me how to get to
the supermarket?

Speaker 1:   Tomorrow there will be a test in
class, so you don't need your textbooks. But
please bring a number 2 pencil.

Speaker 2:   As you read, look for the most
important ideas. Underline the important
points, or use a highlighter so you can see
the information easily.

Speaker 3:   I'll be giving you a lot of handouts
during the class, so make sure that you
have a place to keep them, like a three-ring
binder. You need to keep your notes and
papers organized.

Speaker 4:   For the presentations tomorrow,
please bring your presentation on a
flash drive so that we can put it on the
class computer.

Speaker 5:   When you're giving your
presentations, don't read from your
notebook. Write your main points on index
cards: one card for each main point. That
way it's easier for you to remember what you
have to say.

UNIT 5

▶ **Burj Khalifa**

This is the Burj Khalifa in Dubai in the United
Arab Emirates. It's the world's tallest building.
It's more than half a mile, or over 800
meters, tall.

The Burj Khalifa is taller than any other
building in the world, but it has one
problem—its windows still get dirty.

These are the men who clean the world's
highest windows. They work thousands of
feet above the ground every day.

Johnny Salvador is the manager of a team of 15
people who clean the Burj's 24,000 windows.

When they are working, the men have to be
very careful. It's very windy, and the winds are
the strongest at the top.

Johnny's team must work for three months to
clean all of the windows of the Burj Khalifa. It's
a dangerous but exciting job.

has to
have to
should

I have to choose a course.
Should I be a musician?
He has to get some advice.
You have to work hard.
I should go to medical school.
She has to decide what to do.

Advisor: Come in!

Beatrice: Hello! It's, uh, I'm Beatrice.

Advisor: Ah, yes, Beatrice! Please, come in.
Take a seat.

Beatrice: Thank you.

Advisor: So, how can I help you?

Beatrice: Well, I'm going to college next year.

Advisor: Uh-huh.

Beatrice: I have to choose a major ... but I don't know what to do. I need your **advice**. Should I go to medical school, or should I go to music school? Should I be a doctor? A musician? Should I go to engineering school and become an engineer?

Advisor: Hmm. Those are good questions. Tell me about music school.

Beatrice: Well, there aren't many **jobs** for musicians. Well, OK, I'm sorry. That's not true. There are a lot of jobs in music—but it's a **hard** life. They **work** hard, but many musicians don't **earn** a lot of money.

Advisor: I see. And what about medical school?

Beatrice: Well, a doctor's life ... Wow! It's a good job. It's not **boring**, and you can earn good money and **help** people.

Advisor: Yes, that's true.

Beatrice: But ... I don't know. Medical school's difficult. You have to work hard.

Advisor: Hmm. What do your parents say?

Beatrice: Well, my mother thinks I should go to medical school.

Advisor: Why?

Beatrice: Oh, because my grades are good. I have good grades in science and English.

Advisor: And what about your father?

Beatrice: Well, he says I can be a doctor or an engineer or, well, anything I guess. What do you think? What should I do?

Advisor: Well, you're a good student, and you have good grades. But for now, I think you should get a job.

Beatrice: What? Why?

Advisor: Well, I don't think you should go to college now because you don't know if you want to be a musician or a doctor ... or an engineer! I think you should get a job. Then you can go to college later when you know what ...

🔊 5.4
1 Fatima has two jobs.
2 Mark has to work very hard.
3 I have a very good job.
4 Engineers have a difficult job.
5 Paul has an important job.
6 Builders have to work fast.

🔊 5.5
1 boring
2 interesting
3 safe
4 easy
5 difficult
6 nice
7 big
8 small
9 fast
10 important

🔊 5.6
Paul: Morning, Emma! And how are you today?
Emma: I'm fine thanks, Paul.
Paul: Good, good. Now then—what do you have for me here?
Emma: Well, here are two people for the job at the sports center.
Paul: I see. Which job is this? Is it for the fitness instructor? Or for the sports-center nurse?
Emma: This is for the fitness instructor. We're going to look at people for the nurse's job next week.
Paul: Ah, next week. OK, I see. So, who's this?
Emma: Well, this is Alan Green.
Paul: Ah, I see he's an American.
Emma: Yes. What do you think?
Paul: Well, he's **strong** and **in shape** ... and he does a lot of sports: Soccer, basketball, karate, judo. That's great.
Emma: But ... ?

Paul: But he's a student. I think a good fitness instructor should be a good teacher. I want a person who has experience—a person who can **teach** me tennis or volleyball.

Emma: OK, well, here's Lucy Lau.

Paul: Hmm. Ah, good! She's a sports scientist ... and she's a fitness instructor! That's great! So, I think Lucy is our new fitness instructor. What do you think?

Emma: Well ...

Paul: You're not sure?

Emma: Lucy is very good. But I think a fitness instructor has to be strong and in great shape. I think he—or she—has to be a good **example** for the students.

Paul: Interesting, go on.

Emma: We want a person who can make the students work hard. Lucy says, "It is important to be **kind** and **polite**." That's a good idea. But if you want to get in shape, you have to work hard. I think Alan can help people do that.

Paul: I see, I see. But I think we should choose Lucy. She teaches zumba, pilates, and yoga— and these are very popular right now.

Emma: Mm, that's true. Would you like me to write to Lucy and tell her the good news?

Paul: Yes, I think that would be ...

🔊 5.7

stronger
faster
harder
safer
kinder

🔊 5.8

Conversation 1

Carla: Professor, may I please speak to you for a moment?

Professor: Yes, of course, Carla. What's up?

Carla: Well ... I have a problem. Em ... my sister is getting married next month in Florida.

Professor: Aha.

Carla: And ... I have to go to the wedding. So ... I'm going to miss some classes.

Professor: Hmm. How many classes will you miss?

Carla: Well ... Probably two. One on Friday April 8 and another one on Monday April 11.

Professor: Well, I guess that's OK. Thank you for letting me know ... But please don't miss any more classes this semester.

Carla: I won't.

Professor: And, Carla ... could you please tell me again in a couple of weeks? I can give you some reading to do.

Carla: Yes, OK. Thank you very much, professor!

Conversation 2

Administrator: Hi, how can I help you?

Selma: Uh ... is this the tutoring center?

Administrator: Yes, that's right. What do you need?

Selma: Um ... I'd like to work with a tutor, if possible. I'm having problems with my writing.

Administrator: Well ... the earliest I have available is Wednesday. Can you do 10:30 on Wednesday?

Selma: Oh, I can't come at that time. I have a class. Is it possible to come later?

Administrator: Uh ... how about 12:15?

Selma: Yes, I can do that.

Administrator: OK. Let's make it for 12:15. Can you give me your name?

Selma: Yes, it's Selma ... S ... E ... L ... .M ... A Chen. C ... H ... E ... N,

Administrator: OK, Selma. Come back to this office at 12:15 on Wednesday.

Selma: Great! Thank you.

UNIT 6

▶ **Monticello and Jefferson**

This beautiful building is Monticello, in Virginia. It's the home of Thomas Jefferson, the third President of the United States, from 1797 to 1801. He is very important to Americans because he wrote the Declaration of Independence.

He lived in this house in Virginia, United States. The house has 33 rooms. And it's an important, interesting part of American history.

It took more than 40 years for Jefferson to finish building Monticello, in 1809. He wanted to build a home that looked different for his new country. So he combined Italian, English, and French styles.

When you go through the front door, you enter the Indian Hall. On the walls, there are many Native American and hunting items from the new world.

But in other rooms, like this one, the styles are from European cultures.

Also on the first floor is Jefferson's private area, including his bedroom and study. He wanted his house to be convenient and comfortable.

When he got out of bed in the morning, he could go directly into his study and start working—on science, farming, or politics. Monticello also had 5,000 acres of land, with many gardens and a large working farm.

Today it is a living museum—a memory of early American history.

🔊 6.1

1 an author of many books
2 I help architects.
3 For example
4 good ideas
5 restaurants in Los Angeles
6 What about the U.S.?

🔊 6.2

Paul: Good evening. I'm Paul Clark, and welcome to *Think Design*. I have a special guest today—Dr. Kay Thompson. Dr. Thompson is a psychologist and an author of many books. Welcome, Dr. Thompson. Now, you're not an architect, but you help design buildings. What do you do?

Dr. Thompson: Well, I help architects choose good colors for their buildings.

Paul: Is color important?

Dr. Thompson: Yes. Very important. Why? Because color can change the way we think, the way we feel, even the way we talk.

Paul: Really?

Dr. Thompson: Yes. For example, many restaurants in Mexico have orange **walls**.

Paul: Why?

Dr. Thompson: Well, what do you think?

Paul: Oh, um, I don't know, er, is orange a warm color? Is it a friendly color?

Dr. Thompson: Those are good ideas. But, no. The walls are orange because some experts think that orange makes people feel hungry.

Paul: Hungry? How interesting! But ... is that true? You don't see many orange restaurants in Los Angeles, for example. Why is that?

Dr. Thompson: Because colors mean different things in different countries. For example, if you go on the Internet and look for photographs of "Chinese restaurants," you're going to see a lot of red! Red walls, red **floors**, maybe even red **ceilings**!

Paul: Why? Do they think that red makes people feel hungry?

Dr. Thompson: Good question, but no. Many Chinese restaurants are red because in China red is the color of fire, of happiness, and of all the good things in life.

Paul: I see. This is really interesting. So what about the United States? If my friend opens a restaurant, what color should it be?

Dr. Thompson: Well, if you mean traditional American food, white is a good color—white and also a **wood** color in a **room**.

Paul: Oh? Why?

Dr. Thompson: Because natural things are important to many people in the U.S. White means fresh and clean, and the wood colors—brown, yellow—are natural. And nature is healthy.

Paul: I see, so **furniture** must be important, too. If the tables and chairs are traditional or new, for example.

Dr. Thompson: Well, that's another ...

🔊 **6.3**

armchair, table, chair, bookcase, lamp, desk, sofa

🔊 **6.4**

comfortable, glass, leather, metal, plastic, uncomfortable, wooden

🔊 **6.5**

Dale: ... thanks for the coffee, Hakan! Very nice!

Hakan: Yes, it's good Turkish coffee. OK, then. Should we start?

Dale: Yes, I think so. OK, so we need a place for our new office. What about here?

Hakan: Where?

Dale: Downtown. What do you think?

Hakan: Well, it's a good place. It's **near** some good roads. But ... I don't think we should go there.

Dale: Oh? Why not?

Hakan: Because the buildings downtown are very old. They are cold in winter and hot in summer, and they're very **noisy**. They're uncomfortable places.

Dale: Oh, I see. That's not good.

Hakan: No. And the buildings there are **expensive**.

Dale: Really?

Hakan: Yes. My sister's a lawyer, and her office is downtown. She likes her job, but she does not like her building.

Dale: OK, so not there, then! Hmm. What about here?

Hakan: The park?

Dale: Yes. It's **quiet**, and it's not **far** from a big road. What do you think?

Hakan: Hmm, I'm not sure. It's pretty far from the town. What about here? Near the train station?

Dale: The train station is good. It's good for travel ... but I think we should go to the park. The buildings near the train station aren't **cheap**.

Hakan: They're not?

Dale: No. They're really expensive.

Hakan: OK, let's go with the park. I'm happy with that. Now, what about the design? I think we should have a **modern** design with big windows. What about you?

Dale: Yes, I agree. Big windows are good. What about the walls? What color do you think we should paint the walls?

Hakan: Hmm. What about blue?

Dale: Blue's a good color, but I'm not sure. Blue can make people feel cold.

Hakan: Ah, yes, that's true. What about yellow? Because it's a warm and sunny color.

Dale: Yes, you're right. Yellow's a good color. OK, so what's next? Ah, OK, furniture. So what do you think?

Hakan: Well, I think we should have modern desks and chairs. The desks can be made of metal and wood. Then, we can have comfortable chairs. It will all be new and beautiful.

1

Dale: ... OK, so we need a place for our new office. What about here?

Hakan: Where?

Dale: Downtown. What do you think?

Hakan: Well, it's a good place. It's near some good roads. But ... I don't think we should go there.

Dale: Oh? Why not?

Hakan: Because the buildings downtown are very old. They are cold in winter and hot in summer, and they're very noisy. They're uncomfortable places.

2

Dale: What about here?

Hakan: The park?

Dale: Yes. It's quiet, and it's not far from a big road. What do you think?

Hakan: Hmm, I'm not sure. It's pretty far from the town. What about here? Near the train station?

Dale: The train station is good. It's good for travel ... but I think we should go to the park. The buildings near the train station aren't cheap.

3

Hakan: Now, what about the design? I think we should have big windows. What about you?

Dale: Yes, I agree. Big windows are good.

🔊 6.7

Professor: Sam, could I have a word with you for a moment?

Sam: Er ... yes.

Professor: I wanted to ask you about the class. Is everything OK for you?

Sam: Yes, thank you. I like the class.

Professor: Is the material too difficult? Do you understand everything?

Sam: Er ... Yes ... yes, I do. It's fine.

Professor: OK ... Well ... it's just that ... I notice that you don't participate in class very much. Today I noticed ... you were falling asleep at one point!

Sam: I'm sorry, Professor. I went to bed late last night.

Professor: Well, maybe you should go to bed earlier.

Sam: I know. I'm sorry.

Professor: And, anyway, it's not only today. You often look at your cell phone.

Sam: Oh ... yes. I was using my dictionary.

Professor: OK ... But ... the thing is ... if you don't participate more in class, your grade will go down.

Sam: My grade will go down? But ... I got an A on my paper.

Professor: I know. Your written work is good, and your grades are good right now. But part of your grade is for class participation.

Sam: You mean ... ? Sorry, I don't really understand.

Professor: Well, I need to see that you are paying attention in class, and thinking about the material.

Sam: Oh ... I see.

Professor: And I need you to speak up more in class. Ask questions.

Sam: OK.

Professor: Especially in group work. When you're in a group with other students.

Sam: Yes.

Professor: OK. So remember that. And I'll see you tomorrow.

Sam: Thank you, Professor.

UNIT 7

▶ Eating Insects

Today this reporter is visiting an elementary school in Thailand. It's in the middle of rice farms and coconut trees. He's interested in food in other cultures.

Eating habits start when we are very young. Maybe that's why people in some cultures like to eat insects.

Mrs. Noi, the school principal, invited the reporter to help cook lunch for the students. And what are they going to eat? Insects! Every evening, the students have to do their homework, but they also have to catch tomorrow's lunch. Now it's time to get to work in the kitchen.

First they put the insects in hot oil. Then they add special leaves from local plants. Then they fry everything in a big pan so it is safe to eat. The food looks strange to the reporter, but, when he tastes it, it tastes pretty normal—like chicken-flavored potato chips.

Lunch is very popular with the students. These children eat insects every day, so it's not unusual for them. In fact, they love it!

◀) 7.1

Fif-teen thousand dollars every month?

Se-ven-teen million?

Sorry—how many children? Six-teen?

We feed six-ty children from poor families here. Fifty? No, six-ty.

◀) 7.2

1

Speaker A: Is the number of people there about seventy million?

Speaker B: Um, no, I think it's about seventeen.

Speaker A: Seventeen million? OK, thanks.

2

Speaker A: We feed sixty children from poor families here.

Speaker B: Sorry—how many children? Sixteen?

Speaker A: No, sixty.

3

Speaker A: Thirteen percent of this class are vegetarians—people who don't eat meat.

Speaker B: Thirty? Are you sure?

Speaker A: No, no—thirteen!

4

Speaker A: People in this city eat fifteen thousand tons of beef every month.

Speaker B: Is that true? Fifty thousand tons every month?

Speaker A: No, fifteen thousand—not fifty.

◀) 7.3

Professor: OK, everyone. So tonight I'd like to talk about traditions and food in the past and present. For example, in the past, **meat** was expensive or was not available. My grandparents only had meat on special holidays. But now, in the U.S., meat is always available. Americans eat meat about 218 times a year. Are meat **dishes** as special now? How about in your family? Yes, Raki?

Raki: Well, my grandparents ate a lot of **fish**.

Professor: Uh-huh, where did they live?

Raki: In Japan. They lived by the water, so it was easy to get. Everyone ate fish, and **rice** and **vegetables**. People made our traditional dishes with that.

Professor: Do they still do this today?

Raki: Yeah, but today we have foods from everywhere. Italian food is very popular in Japan now.

Jose: This is the same in my country, Mexico. Fifty years ago, my grandmother cooked traditional dishes at home every day. But now, there are so many **international** foods available in the supermarket, like Middle Eastern, Chinese, or Italian. They're cheap and already prepared, so there's no need to make them.

Professor: Class, do you think these international dishes are like the dishes your grandmother made?

Raki / Jose / Others: No. / No way. / Uh-uh.

Professor: In fact, Jose, do you know how to cook?

Jose: No, I never learned. We moved a lot. My parents both worked, so they didn't cook very much. We ate a lot of **fast food**. You know, burgers and fries. It wasn't very healthy, I know.

Professor: OK, so let me take a quick survey. How many of you know how to cook? ... Uh ... 13, no, only 14 students out of 30?! Wow! Can any of you cook traditional dishes? Hmm ... only 20%! I guess this isn't a surprise. So, what do you think? Now that we have so many foods available from around the world, do you think it's good or bad for our traditions?

🔊 **7.4**

Sophie: Hello. I'm Sophie. This afternoon, I'm going to tell you the results of my survey. My questions were on the topic of food and **culture** in France. I think this is an interesting topic. There were three questions in my survey.

The French love food, and it's very important to them. So, my first question was, "Do they eat a lot of fast food in France?" I learned something really surprising. The French eat a lot of fast food, in fact it's their **favorite** food for eating out. You can see here that 54% of all restaurant sales were from fast food places. I didn't know it was so popular. In one survey I read, in the past, people had 80 minutes for lunch and now only 22 minutes. Because lunches are shorter, people can't go home for **home-cooked meals**, so they eat fast food. I also read that more people eat alone or at their desks than they did before. My second question was, "Is eating together with others

important?" For most, 80% of the people, meals are still a time to eat and talk together. My last question was, "How do the French feel about food?" Scientists believe that feeling good about food is better for your health. So, when you look here, 84% of the people in France **enjoy** food. The taste is very important for French people. They eat **healthy** foods like fresh fruits, vegetables, fish, meats, and breads. Even fast food restaurants have to make meals that taste better than usual. Well, I wasn't surprised by that! Like everywhere, fast food is cheaper and easier for workers. So, my conclusion is, fast food is changing some traditions about eating in France. What do you think? Is fast food good or bad for our meal-time traditions?

🔊 **7.5**

Sophie: Hello. I'm Sophie. This afternoon, I'm going to tell you the results of my survey. My questions were on the topic of food and culture in France. I think this is an interesting topic. There were three questions in my survey.

🔊 **7.6**

Tomoko: Good morning! I'm Tomoko. I'm going to tell you about the results of my survey. There were five questions in my survey. My topic was traditional Japanese food. I think this is an interesting topic.

Ahmed: Hello, everybody! I'm Ahmed. I'm going to tell you about the results of my survey. My topic was fast food in Abu Dhabi. There were three questions in my survey. I think this is a good topic.

🔊 **7.7**

question   survey   result   U.S.   popular

🔊 7.8

1 I'm going to tell you about the results of my survey.
2 There were four questions about food and culture.
3 Are fast food restaurants popular?
4 People had 80 minutes for lunch.

🔊 7.9

1 So, my first question was, "Do they eat a lot of fast food in France?"
2 You can see here that 54% percent of all restaurant sales were from fast food places.
3 In one survey I read, in the past, people had 80 minutes for lunch and now only 22 minutes.
4 My second question was "Is eating together with others important?"
5 My last question was, "How do the French feel about food?"
6 So when you look here, 84% of the people in France enjoy food …

🔊 7.10

Speaker 1: Do I have a healthy lifestyle? Well … I think I do. I have a really busy schedule. But I eat pretty well because I live with my family, and my grandmother cooks dinner for me most evenings. She's a great cook, and she cooks a lot of vegetables … not so much red meat. I usually take some food for lunch the next day, so I don't buy a lot of snacks … and I never drink soda. I drink water. I know I don't get enough exercise. I love to work out, but it's very hard to find time during the semester. I'm taking four classes, and I have a job. I usually go to bed early, because I have to get up early to take the bus.

Speaker 2: A healthy lifestyle? Erm … No. Not really! I live on campus, so I have to eat in the cafeteria. I really don't like the food there. The best thing they have are the hamburgers—they're really good, so I eat them a lot. The other thing I like is pizza. We get pizza a couple of times a week. I know I don't eat enough vegetables … Exercise? Well … I do get exercise. Most days I play basketball with my friends. It's great if you're feeling stressed out: you play a game, and you forget everything. After that, I usually drink an energy drink. It gives me energy for my evening classes! I don't have a problem sleeping, but I usually go to bed late. And I sometimes stay up all night to finish a paper.

UNIT 8

▶ China's Modern Roadways

More people have cars now than ever before. And the number is growing all the time.

As a result, there are also more roads than ever before. From Great Britain to Dubai, from the USA to Mexico, roads and highways will take you anywhere you want to go.

At the moment, China is constructing more roads than any other country in the world.

In 1989, China had fewer than 100 miles of highways. Now it has more than 50,000.

That's more than the United States, which has 47,000 miles of interstate highways.

In the middle of China, you can find one of the world's greatest roads.

It's called the G50.

The G50 is almost 1,200 miles long, and it connects the middle of China to the port city of Shanghai on the east coast.

It was difficult to build, but nothing could stop it. One minute you're driving through the middle of a mountain. The next minute you're driving in the air. This amazing highway also includes the world's highest bridge.

It's not this one.

It's this one, the Sidu Bridge.

The Sidu Bridge is more than 1,500 feet above the ground. It's so high that you could put the Empire State Building under it!

🔊 8.1

1238; 1868; 1923; 1996; 2005

🔊 8.2

1435; 1749; 1949; 1953; 2017

🔊 8.3

Steve: Hi! Good morning! Thank you for asking me here today. OK, so my name's Steve, and I work for Transport for London. Today I'm going to tell you about the work we do and especially tell you about the electronic **tickets** we use in London.

OK, so what do we do at Transport for London? Well, we take care of travelers in London. This can be people who **travel** on private transportation or public transportation. Three million people travel in private cars and **taxis**, and another five million use the **bus**, **trains**, and, of course, the famous London Underground—which is the name of the world's oldest **subway**. So that's a total of around eight million people.

Student: How old is it?

Steve: Sorry? What was that?

Student: How old is the London Underground?

Steve: Ah! Oh, uh, it's more than 150 years old. It opened in 1863.

Student: Thanks.

Steve: Sure. So, Transport for London started in 2000, and, in 2003, we introduced the Oyster card. It's an electronic ticket system. Before Oyster cards, people had to buy paper tickets. And that was OK when fewer people lived and worked in London. They could buy tickets for one **trip** or for a day or for a month. But there was a problem—it was very slow.

Student: Why? How did people use tickets before?

Steve: Each **passenger** waited to buy a ticket, and then they went to the gate. At the gate, they put the ticket into the machine. Then the gate opened, and then they took their ticket from the machine. Now, this took a long time, and more people started to live and work in London, so we needed a faster ticket system. And this was the Oyster card. You can pay for your trips online and walk through the gates much faster. Now, you can also use your credit card. You just tap your card. The result? It's very fast and easy. Many people are using this way to …

🔊 8.4

Teacher: OK, so work with your partner. Five minutes!

Iman: Hi, hello. I'm sorry. What's your name?

Anna: Oh, I'm Anna.

Iman: Anna? OK, and I'm Iman. Can I go first?

Anna: Yes, sure. What's your topic?

Iman: Transportation in cities: **problems** and solutions. OK, so I'm going to start with some facts about life in cities. More and more people are living in cities than in the countryside. This means that cities have a lot of **traffic** problems because many people use their cars to go to work or school or shop … or whatever. With all of these cars, it takes more time *and* **gas** to travel around the city. This is expensive for people, and the pollution is very bad in some places. What's more, being in a car for a long time can be dangerous because drivers get tired. So, what is the solution?

Some cities think that **bikes** are a good **idea**, so they have free bikes for people to use. Other cities have carpooling. With carpooling, more people ride together in one car, so there aren't as many cars. There's another new idea that's interesting. It's a self-driving car. That's right! The driver doesn't have to drive the car! And, because there are a lot of bad drivers, it can help stop **accidents**. Now in the city of Dubai, they are working hard to find solutions for their traffic problems because there are too many cars. They plan to build a subway—like the one in London—so there will be fewer cars on the road. Another thing is people don't like to walk on the **sidewalks** outside. It's too hot! So a big shopping mall there has an inside sidewalk that moves! Nice, huh? It's air-conditioned and goes from the mall to the train station and other places near the mall. It's not short either. It takes 15–20 minutes to walk it, so people get exercise, feel comfortable, and—more importantly—don't drive. These are some solutions some cities …

🔊 8.5

Iman: More and more people are living in cities than in the countryside. This means that cities have a lot of traffic problems because many people use their cars to go to work or school or shop … or whatever. With all of these cars, it takes more time *and* gas to travel around the city. This is expensive for people, and the pollution is very bad in some places.

🔊 8.6

Steve: Each passenger waited to buy a ticket, and then they went to the gate. At the gate, they put the ticket into the machine. Then the gate opened, and then they took their ticket from the machine. Now, this took a long time, and more people started to live and work in London, so we needed a faster ticket system. And this was the Oyster card.

🔊 8.7

happened; changed; visited; guessed; needed; waited; asked; helped; showed; watched; opened; started

🔊 8.8

Interviewer: Good morning, and welcome to the show. Today's interview is with Professor Ken Davidson. He's a psychologist, and he is director of the Student Success Center at State College. Welcome to the program.

Davidson: Thank you.

Interviewer: First, can you tell me a little bit about what you do?

Davidson: Yes. The Student Success Center gives help to students who need it.

Interviewer: You mean, help with their classes?

Davidson: Well, not really. We mainly provide counseling—someone to talk to if you need help with personal problems, or …

Interviewer: What are the most common difficulties that students have?

Davidson: Probably the most common problem is stress. Many students feel overwhelmed. They feel that they have too much to do and too little time.

Interviewer: Mm. Why is this? Why are students so overwhelmed these days?

Davidson: Well, many students are working while they are in college. They have jobs. Some students have families as well. When they begin college, they have to manage all of that at the same time.

Interviewer: So how do you help them?

Davidson: Well … we can help them to plan their schedule. We have workshops on time management strategies. We try to teach students to use their time better.

Interviewer: I see. What other kinds of problems do you see?

Davidson: Well, sometimes a student is in a bad relationship … maybe with a friend or a roommate … even a teacher. So a counselor might help them to talk about it and decide what to do.

Interviewer: Mm. What advice do you have for students who are having these kinds of problems?

Davidson: Well, the first thing is to understand that there is a problem. Often, students don't think that they need help. They just say, "Oh, I'm fine!" But you can't do well in college if you are unhappy.

Interviewer: Right.

Davidson: And the second thing is to ask for help! There are many people on campus who can help you, but you have to ask.

Interviewer: So … students shouldn't feel bad about … feeling bad!

Davidson: No! It's normal to feel stressed and overwhelmed sometimes.

Interviewer: Thank you very much for speaking with us, Professor.

Davidson: It's a pleasure. Thank you.

The authors and publishers acknowledge the following sources of copyright material and are grateful for the permissions granted. While every effort has been made, it has not always been possible to identify the sources of all the material used, or to trace all copyright holders. If any omissions are brought to our notice, we will be happy to include the appropriate acknowledgements on reprinting and in the next update to the digital edition, as applicable.

Photo credits

Key: T = Top, C = Center, B = Below, L = Left, R = Right, TL = Top Left, TR = Top Right, BL = Below Left, BR = Below Right.

p. 12: Cultura RM Exclusive/Peter Muller/Getty Images; pp. 14–15: Derek Meijer/Alamy; p. 18 (L): ZouZou1/iStock/Getty Images; p. 18 (R): Jochen Schlenker/robertharding/Getty Images; p. 21: Tom Merton/Caiaimage/Getty Images; p. 25 (photo a): Frederick M. Brown/Stringer/Getty Images Entertainment/Getty Images; p. 25 (photo b): Neilson Barnard/Getty Images Entertainment/Getty Images; p. 25 (photo c), p. 27 (L): Kimberly White/Stringer/Getty Images Entertainment/Getty Images; p. 25 (photo d): Paul Morigi/Stringer/Getty Images Entertainment/Getty Images; p. 25 (photo e): Michael Buckner/Getty Images Entertainment/Getty Images; p. 25 (photo f): Ben Gabbe/Getty Images Entertainment/Getty Images; p. 27 (R), p. 176 (photo d): Bloomberg/Getty Images; p. 34 (photo 1): Ariel Skelley/Blend Images/Getty Images; p. 34 (photo 2): kali9/iStock/Getty Images Plus/Getty Images; pp. 36–37: Warren Faidley/Corbis/Getty Images; p. 41 (photo a), p. 43 (TL): AmyKerk/iStock/Getty Images; p. 41 (photo b), p. 43 (TR): Stephen J Krasemann/All Canada Photos/Getty Images; p. 41 (photo c), p. 43 (BL): Per Breiehagen/Photographer's Choice/Getty Images; p. 41 (photo d), p. 43 (BR): emholk/iStock/Getty Images; p. 47 (photo a): Design Pics Inc/Perspectives/Getty Images; p. 47 (photo b): Ed Norton/Lonely Planet Images/Getty Images; p. 47 (photo c): Allan Johnson/EyeEm/Getty Images; p. 51 (L), p. 52 (L): prasit chansarekorn/E+/Getty Images; p. 51 (R), p. 52 (R): Benjamin Torode/Moment/Getty Images; p. 56: Trish Punch/Lonely Planet Images/Getty Images; pp. 58–59: Tim Graham/Getty Images News/Getty Images; p. 62 (photo a): Pamela Moore/iStock/Getty Images; p. 62 (photo b): ColorBlind Images/The Image Bank/Getty Images; p. 62 (photo c): Wavebreakmedia Ltd/Getty Images; p. 63 (photo d): JFB/Stone/Getty Images; p. 63 (photo e): Mike Harrington/DigitalVision/Getty Images; p. 63 (photo f): Betsie Van Der Meer/Taxi/Getty Images; p. 63 (photo g): Robert Daly/Caiaimage/Getty Images; p. 65: Hero Images/Getty Images; p. 69: Maisant Ludovic/hemis.fr/Getty Images; p. 70: Cathy Yeulet/Hemera/Getty Images; p. 71: Marc Romanelli/Blend Images/Getty Images; p. 75: andresr/E+/Getty Images; p. 78: PeopleImages/E+/Getty Images; pp. 80–81: Cultura RM Exclusive/Christoffer Askman/Getty Images; p. 100 (photo a): Sean Macdiarmid/Hemera/Getty Images Plus/Getty Images; p. 100 (photo b): filipfoto/iStock/Getty Images Plus/Getty Images; p. 100 (photo c): RAstem GRLER/E+/Getty Images; p. 100 (photo d): BrianAJackson/iStock/Getty Images Plus/Getty Images; p. 100 (photo e): kelifamily/iStock/Getty Images Plus/Getty Images; p. 100 (photo f): Wavebreak Media/Getty Images Plus/Getty Images; p. 100 (photo g): Samuel Kessler/E+/Getty Images; p. 100 (photo h): Don Farrall/Photodisc/Getty Images; pp. 102–103: Purestock/Getty Images; p. 116 (L), p. 195 (L): imagenavi/Getty Images; p. 116 (R), p. 193 (L): Jupiterimages/Getty Images; p. 119 (T), p. 121 (L): DreamPictures/Blend Images/Getty Images; p. 119 (C), p. 121 (C): Jose Luis Pelaez Inc/Blend Images/Getty Images; p. 119 (B), p. 121 (R): Susan Vogel/UpperCut Images/Getty Images; p. 124: Hisayoshi Osawa/DigitalVision/Getty Images; pp. 126–127: Peter Adams/Photolibrary/Getty Images; p. 133 (armchair): Onur Döngel/E+/Getty Images; p. 133 (table): Bulgac/iStock/Getty Images; p. 133 (chair): nuwatphoto/iStock/Getty Images; p. 133 (bookcase): DEA/G. CIGOLINI/De Agostini/Getty mages; p. 133 (lamp): malerapaso/iStock/Getty Images; p. 133 (desk): Spiderstock/E+/Getty Images; p. 133 (sofa): BLUEXHAND/iStock/Getty Images; p. 138 (L), p. 142 (L): Christian Heeb/AWL Images/Getty Images; p. 138 (C), p. 142 (C): Bruno De Hogues/Stockbyte/Getty Images; p. 138 (R), p. 142 (R): View Pictures/Universal Images Group/Getty Images; p. 146 (L): Compassionate Eye Foundation/Chris Ryan/Taxi/Getty Images; p. 146 (R): skynesher/E+/Getty Images; pp. 148–149: Richard I'Anson/Lonely Planet Images/Getty Images; p. 157 (photo a): Thomas Firak Photography/Photographer's Choice/Getty Images; p. 157 (photo b): Dorling Kindersley/Getty Images; p. 157 (photo c): carlosgaw/E+/Getty Images; p. 157 (photo d): Lilechka75/iStock/Getty Images; p. 157 (photo e): Elena Danileiko/iStock/Getty Images; p. 157 (photo f): TAGSTOCK1/iStock/Getty Images; p. 157 (photo g): ElNariz/iStock/Getty Images; p. 157 (photo h): OksanaKiian/iStock/Getty Images; p. 168 (photo 1): Matilde Gattoni/arabianEye/Getty Images; p. 168 (photo 2): Image Source/Getty Images; p. 168 (photo 3): PeopleImages.com/Getty Images; pp. 170–171: Ellen van Bodegom/Moment/Getty Images; p. 176 (photo a): Travelpix Ltd/Photographer's Choice/Getty Images; p. 176 (photo b): geotrac/iStock/Getty Images; p. 176 (photo c): inFocusDC/iStock/Getty Images; p. 176 (photo e): helovi/iStock/Getty Images; p. 188 (L): Kevin Dodge/Blend Images/Getty Images; p. 188 (R): Juanmonino/E+/Getty Images; p. 190: Diane Diederich/Vetta/Getty Images; p. 193 (R): Hiroyuki Matsumoto/Photographer's Choice/Getty Images; p. 195 (R): Mitch Diamond/Photodisc/Getty Images.

Front cover photographs by (girl) BestPhotoStudio/Shutterstock and (BG) Andrei Medvedev/Shutterstock.

Illustrations

by Ben Hasler (NB Illustrations) p. 19, 107 (a, c, e, f), 113 (engineer), 113 (musician); Oxford Designers & Illustrators: p. 44, 45, 85, 88, 89, 91, 92, 107 (b, d), 113 (chef), 136, 139, 178, 181, 183; Fiona Gowen: p. 87, 98, 99, 192, 194.

Video stills supplied by BBC Worldwide Learning.

Video supplied by BBC Worldwide Learning.

Corpus

Development of this publication has made use of the Cambridge English Corpus (CEC). The CEC is a multi-billion word computer database of contemporary spoken and written English. It includes British English, American English, and other varieties of English. It also includes the Cambridge Learner Corpus, developed in collaboration with the University of Cambridge ESOL Examinations. Cambridge University Press has built up the CEC to provide evidence about language use that helps to produce better language teaching materials

Cambridge Dictionaries

Cambridge dictionaries are the world's most widely used dictionaries for learners of English. The dictionaries are available in print and online at dictionary.cambridge.org. Copyright © Cambridge University Press, reproduced with permission.

Typeset by emc design ltd

Audio production by CityVox New York

INFORMED BY TEACHERS

Classroom teachers shaped everything about *Prism*. The topics. The exercises. The critical thinking skills. The On Campus sections. Everything. We are confident that *Prism* will help your students succeed in college because teachers just like you helped guide the creation of this series.

Prism Advisory Panel

The members of the *Prism* Advisory Panel provided inspiration, ideas, and feedback on many aspects of the series. *Prism* is stronger because of their contributions.

Gloria Munson
University of Texas, Arlington

Kim Oliver
Austin Community College

Gregory Wayne
Portland State University

Julaine Rosner
Mission College

Dinorah Sapp
University of Mississippi

Christine Hagan
George Brown College/Seneca College

Heidi Lieb
Bergen Community College

Stephanie Kasuboski
Cuyahoga Community College

Global Input

Teachers from more than 500 institutions all over the world provided valuable input through:
- Surveys
- Focus Groups
- Reviews